Office Financials Made Easy

NEW YORK

Published in the United States by LearningExpress, LLC, New York.

Library of Congress Cataloging-in-Publication Data:
Office financials made easy.
p. cm.
ISBN: 978-1-57685-603-1 (alk. paper)
1. Business mathematics. I. LearningExpress (Organization)
HF5691.O39 2008
650.01'513—dc22

2007044435

Printed in the United States of America

9 8 7 6 5 4 3 2 1

First Edition

For more information or to place an order, contact LearningExpress at:
55 Broadway
8th Floor
New York, NY 10006

Or visit us at:
www.learnatest.com

Contents

Introduction

I can remember being in middle and high school thinking I would never need to know the math I was learning at the time. After all, I was not planning on a career in finance or science or anything that I thought would require knowledge of math. After majoring in English literature in college, I found a job in publishing and started my career. However, I soon realized that few people were interested in my thoughts on Henry James. Instead, people wanted me to calculate the earnings before interest and taxes (EBIT) for my department, create new project profit and loss (P&L) statements, and analyze return rates.

I didn't know where to start!

If you are anything like I was, you may not know where to start, either. That is probably why you have picked up this book, *Office Financials Made Easy*. And, luckily for you, this book will show you where to begin with the basic concepts of office math. It will provide an overview of the most common math used in most workplaces and make it simple to understand.

Maybe you have picked up this book because you've been asked to produce a P&L for a new project. Or maybe you've been promoted and now have budgetary responsibilities for your department. Perhaps you recently landed your first job and just want to brush up on your math skills in order to make a good first impression.

It doesn't matter why you've picked up this book. The key is that you want to learn more about the math that you are likely to encounter in a day-to-day office setting. From basic arithmetic like adding, subtracting, multiplying, and dividing to more complex issues like creating an income statement and understanding cash versus accrual accounting, this book will help you understand the business math concepts you need to be successful.

Throughout the book, you'll find quizzes so you can practice your new (or renewed) skills. After you finish a quiz, you can check your answers at the end of the book. You'll also see important workplace tips and memos called out in each

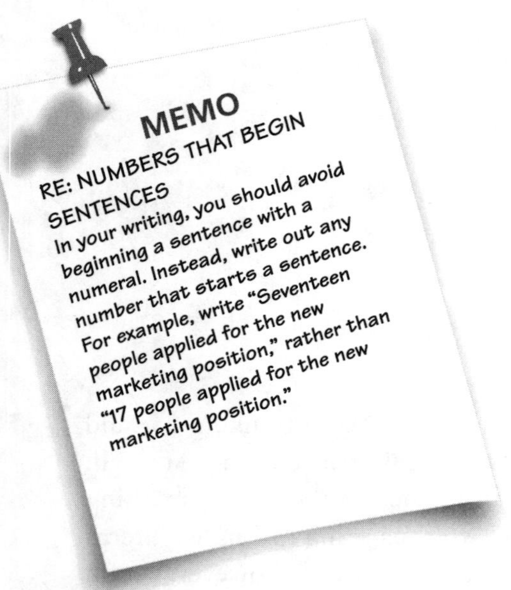

chapter. Pay attention to these, because they contain information to make the application of your business math skills easier.

Now, let's get down to the math at hand. We'll start with the real basics of math and move on from there. Good luck!

PART one

Basic Math Review

CHAPTER ONE

Basic Arithmetic

When you were learning arithmetic in school, you were given problems to solve and paper, pencil, and time to work them out. You were probably encouraged to "show your work" when tackling long division and multiplication. In the workplace, however, you may find that you are faced with math problems that you must solve quickly, in your head. This chapter will provide you with tips and techniques to make the fundamental math processes—addition, subtraction, multiplication, and division—easier for you to manage in your day-to-day duties.

Think of this chapter as a refresher course on the elementary concepts of mathematics. It is not designed to *teach* you how to add, subtract, multiply, and divide. Instead, it is designed to *remind* you how to perform these calculations—and to give you tips on how to calculate them quicker and better.

The mathematics covered in this chapter will prove useful once we move on to harder and more complex issues, such as understanding percentages, calculating payroll, or creating a budget. So,

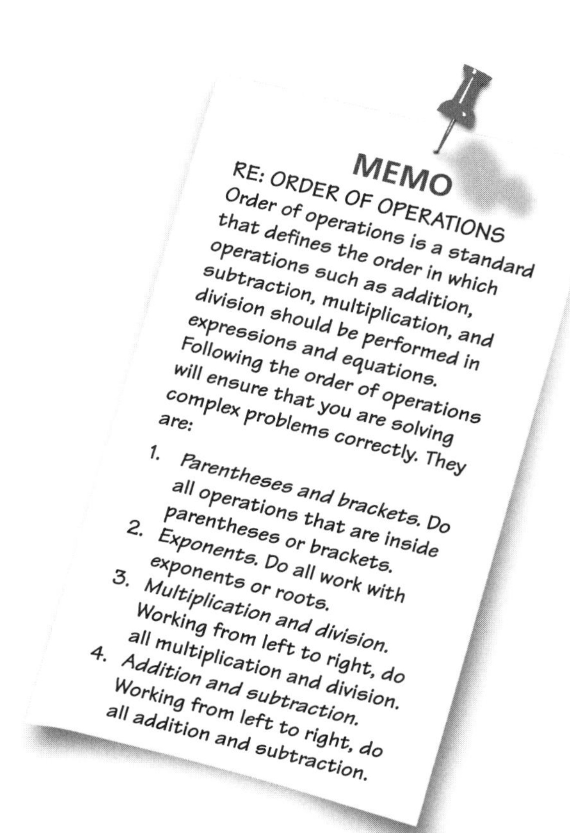

take the time to brush the cobwebs off your math brain, and let's begin by reviewing addition.

ADDITION

Addition, uniting two or more numbers to create a new sum, is the most basic of the arithmetic processes and, therefore, the best place for us to start our review. You probably do most addition without even thinking about it, but there are a few ways by which you can make simple addition easier to do in your head.

The first way to make adding two numbers together easier is by counting up from the larger number. This tip works best when one of the numbers is fairly small. For example, to get the sum for 9 + 4, start with 9 and then count up 4 places to 10, 11, 12, 13, with 13 being the answer.

Here is another example: 387 + 6.

Start with 387 and count up 6 places: 388, 389, 390, 391, 392, 393.

The sum is 393.

For some people, counting up is made possible by using your fingers to keep track of the number that you are counting up. That's okay! Your fingers are a tool, and if they help you arrive at a correct answer more quickly, then use them!

Addition is also easy when one of the numbers is a multiple of 10. If you are adding two or more numbers, and one of them is close to 10 or a multiple of it (10, 20, 30, etc.), then break the other number up to get the first to 10 (or its multiple).

Let's look at this problem: 57 + 14.

The number 57 is 3 away from 60.

Take 3 from 14 and add it to 57. That gives you with 60 + 11, an easier problem to solve.

The sum is 71.

Here is another example that uses 100s instead of 10s: 448 + 95.

The number 95 is 5 away from 100.

Take 5 from 448 and add it to 95 to get 100. This leaves you with 443 + 100, again much easier to solve than 448 + 95.

The sum is 543.

When you are adding larger numbers, there will be many times when you will need to write them down to figure out the sum. Here is a quick overview of the steps involved in adding two numbers, using 424 + 378.

First, stack the numbers and align them on the right. Then, start with the far right column, 4 + 8, to get 12.

$$\begin{array}{r} 424 \\ +\ 378 \\ \hline 2 \end{array}$$

You will have to carry the 1 and add it in the next column, so 2 + 7 becomes 1 + 2 + 7, which equals 10. Carrying a 1 means you now have one "10" added to the 10s column.

$$\begin{array}{r} {\scriptstyle 1} \\ 424 \\ +\ 378 \\ \hline 02 \end{array}$$

Again, carry the 1 and add it in the next column. This last column becomes 1 + 4 + 3 = 8.

$$\begin{array}{r} {\scriptstyle 1\,1} \\ 424 \\ +\ 378 \\ \hline 802 \end{array}$$

So, the answer to the problem is 802.

The best way to get better at addition—or anything, for that matter—is to practice. Be sure to try the problems in the practice quiz to hone your addition skills. Your goal should be to become comfortable enough that you can do most simple addition problems in your head.

MEMO

RE: WHEN IN DOUBT, WRITE IT OUT!

If you can't do a problem in your head, write it out. In the workplace, it is more important to be accurate than to appear like a math whiz. Let's say you are in a meeting and you are asked how many units the sales team needs to sell to reach a quarterly goal. Right now, they've sold 1,527 units and the goal is 3,895. You might be able to do the subtraction in your head, but you might not. So, write it down, subtract 1,527 from 3,895, and feel confident that you will be able to provide the correct answer!

SUBTRACTION

Subtraction, of course, is the opposite of addition. To subtract numbers, line them up just as you would for addition and perform a similar process, except that you subtract instead of adding the numbers. Let's look at 556 – 23. Start with the far right column and subtract 3 from 6:

$$\begin{array}{r} 556 \\ -\ 23 \\ \hline 3 \end{array}$$

Move to the next column and subtract 2 from 5:

$$\begin{array}{r} 556 \\ -\ 23 \\ \hline 33 \end{array}$$

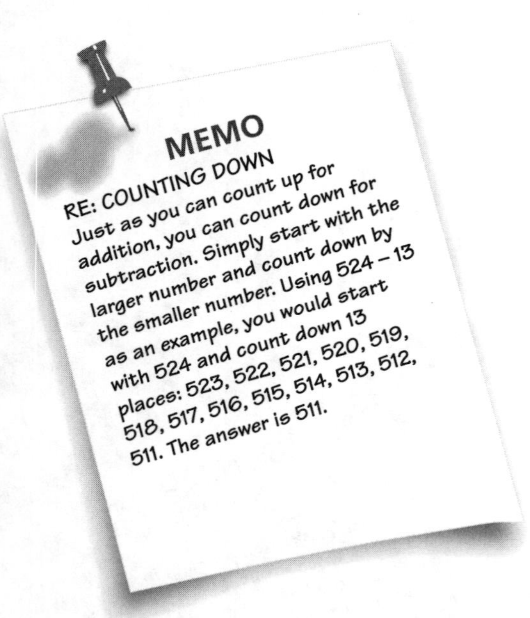

Because there is nothing to subtract from the 5, write that down in the answer.

$$\begin{array}{r} 556 \\ -\ 23 \\ \hline 533 \end{array}$$

The answer to this problem is 533.

Brush up on your skills by working through the problems in the practice quiz at the end of this chapter.

Borrowing

Borrowing, or regrouping, is a technique you can use when you are subtracting one number from another and one column has a smaller number on top. For example, if you line up 726 – 83, you'll see that you will have to subtract 8 from 2:

$$\begin{array}{r} 726 \\ -\ 83 \\ \hline \end{array}$$

First, subtract 3 from 6 in the far right column, to get 3:

$$\begin{array}{r} 726 \\ -\ 83 \\ \hline 3 \end{array}$$

In the next column, you need to subtract 8 from 2. To do this, you need to make the 2 larger by borrowing from the 7, so that the 7 becomes a 6 and the 2 becomes a 12:

$$\begin{array}{r} {\scriptstyle 6\ 12} \\ \not{7}\not{2}6 \\ -\ 83 \\ \hline 3 \end{array}$$

In this example, you are regrouping the top number so that the same quantity—726—is distributed as 6 hundreds, 12 tens, and 6 ones (instead of 7 hundreds, 2 tens, and 6 ones). After you have borrowed, you can finish the problem, subtracting 8 from 12:

$$\begin{array}{r} {\scriptstyle 6\ 12} \\ \not{7}\not{2}6 \\ -\ 83 \\ \hline 43 \end{array}$$

and then bringing the 6 down to the answer:

$$\begin{array}{r} {\scriptstyle 6\ 12} \\ \not{7}\not{2}6 \\ -\ 83 \\ \hline 643 \end{array}$$

When you have a top number that contains zeros, you have to add a step into the borrowing process. Let's look at an example:

$$\begin{array}{r} 503 \\ -\ 46 \\ \hline \end{array}$$

In the first column, you have to subtract 6 from 3, which you can't do unless you borrow from the next column. But, in that column, you have a zero, so there is nothing for you to borrow from. You need to make the zero into a 10 and then you can borrow from it. In this case, you borrow from the 5 to make the zero a 10:

$$\begin{array}{r} {\scriptstyle 4\,10\ } \\ \not{5}\not{0}3 \\ -\ 46 \\ \hline \end{array}$$

Now, you can borrow from the 10 to make the 3 a 13:

$$\begin{array}{r} {\scriptstyle 9\ \ } \\ {\scriptstyle 4\,\not{10}\,13} \\ \not{5}\not{0}\not{3} \\ -\ 46 \\ \hline \end{array}$$

Subtract 6 from 13:

$$\begin{array}{r} {\scriptstyle 9\ \ } \\ {\scriptstyle 4\,\not{10}\,13} \\ \not{5}\not{0}\not{3} \\ -\ 46 \\ \hline 7 \end{array}$$

And then move to the next column and subtract 4 from 9:

$$\begin{array}{r} \scriptstyle 9 \\ \scriptstyle 4\,\cancel{10}\,13 \\ \cancel{503} \\ -\ 46 \\ \hline 57 \end{array}$$

Now, bring the 4 down to the answer:

$$\begin{array}{r} \scriptstyle 9 \\ \scriptstyle 4\,\cancel{10}\,13 \\ \cancel{503} \\ -\ 46 \\ \hline 457 \end{array}$$

When you have multiple zeros in your top number, you would borrow the same way, by regrouping so each zero becomes a 10. Here's an example:

$$\begin{array}{r} 3005 \\ -\ 298 \\ \hline \end{array}$$

You need to borrow to be able to subtract 8 from 5. A quick way to do this is to look at 3,005 as two groups, the 300 and the 5. If you borrow 10 from 300, it becomes 299 and the 5 can become 15, allowing you to subtract 8 from it:

$$\begin{array}{r} \scriptstyle 2\ 9\ 9\ 15 \\ \cancel{3005} \\ -298 \\ \hline 7 \end{array}$$

Since you handled all of the borrowing already, you can continue on with the problem as is, subtracting 9 from 9, then 2 from 9 and, finally, bringing the 2 down to the answer, which is 2,707:

$$\begin{array}{r} {\scriptstyle 2\ 9\ 9\ 15} \\ \cancel{3005} \\ -298 \\ \hline 2707 \end{array}$$

MULTIPLICATION

Multiplication is just shorthand for long addition problems. With multiplication, you are adding a number to itself a set number of times. So, 7×3 means that you are adding $7 + 7 + 7$. Any multiplication problem can be broken down into addition, but that might not always be easy to do. Complex multiplication would take too long to compute if you wrote it out as addition. For example, writing out 244×14 as an addition problem will likely result in nothing more than a hand cramp. Taken as a multiplication problem, however, it is easy to solve.

You will start by multiplying 244×4. Then, multiply 244×10. You finish the problem by adding the results together. The steps follow.

First, as with addition, stack the numbers and align them on the right.

$$\begin{array}{r} 244 \\ \times\ 14 \\ \hline \end{array}$$

Start with the far right column and multiply 4×4. Think of it as $4 + 4 + 4 + 4$ (four 4s added together). You can simplify this mentally by thinking each $4 + 4 = 8$, and then $8 + 8 = 16$. Write down the 6 and remember to carry the 1.

$$\begin{array}{r} {\scriptstyle 1\ } \\ 244 \\ \times\ 14 \\ \hline 6 \end{array}$$

Now, you are faced with 4×4 again. You know it is 16, so add the 1 that you carried to that to get 17. Write down the 7 and carry the 1 again.

$$\begin{array}{r} {}^{1\,1} \\ 244 \\ \times\ 14 \\ \hline 76 \end{array}$$

This last one is simple: $2 \times 4 = 8$. Don't forget that you carried the 1! Add that to the 8 so you have:

$$\begin{array}{r} {}^{1} \\ 244 \\ \times\ 14 \\ \hline 976 \end{array}$$

Now, move on to multiplying 244×10. Write the result below 976. Remember that you are multiplying by 10, even though it looks like you are just multiplying by 1, and place a 0 in the far right position:

$$\begin{array}{r} 244 \\ \times\ 14 \\ \hline 976 \\ 0 \end{array}$$

Now, complete 244×10 to get:

$$\begin{array}{r} 244 \\ \times\ 14 \\ \hline 976 \\ +\ 2440 \\ \hline \end{array}$$

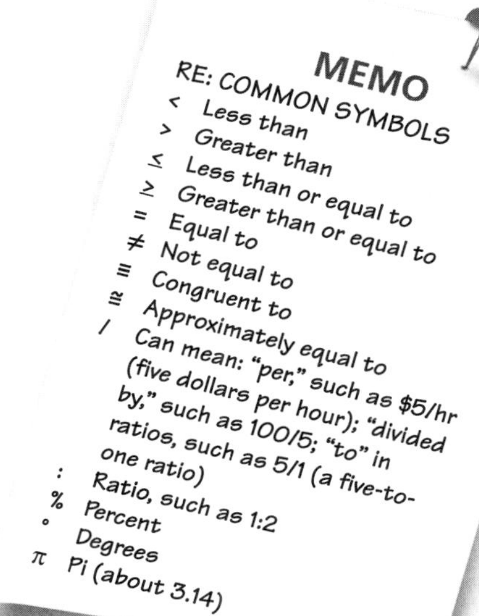

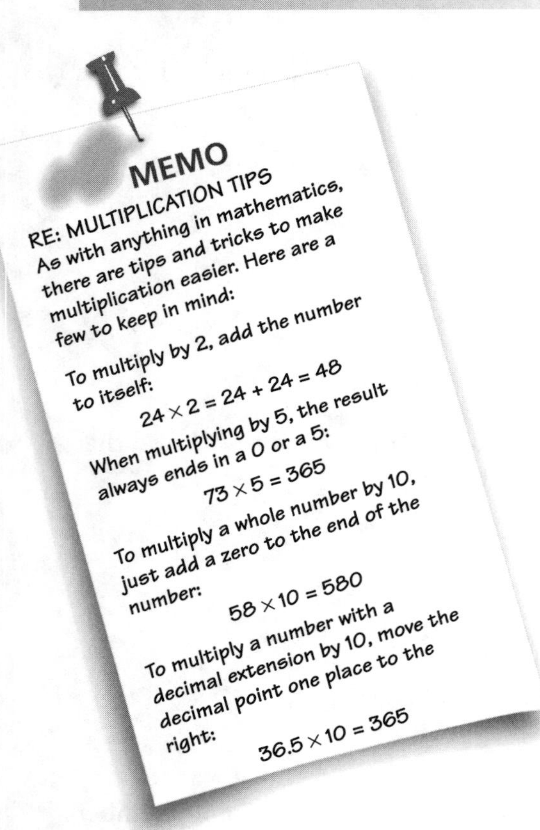

To finish the problem, add the two numbers to find the result, which is 3,416.

$$\begin{array}{r} 244 \\ \times\ 14 \\ \hline 976 \\ +\ 2440 \\ \hline 3416 \end{array}$$

Memorizing the multiplication table will help you conquer the types of multiplication problems you are likely to face in the office. If you can commit the following table to memory, you will have a much easier time multiplying numbers.

THE 12 × MULTIPLICATION TABLE

×	1	2	3	4	5	6	7	8	9	10	11	12
1	1	2	3	4	5	6	7	8	9	10	11	12
2	2	4	6	8	10	12	14	16	18	20	22	24
3	3	6	9	12	15	18	21	24	27	30	33	36
4	4	8	12	16	20	24	28	32	36	40	44	48
5	5	10	15	20	25	30	35	40	45	50	55	60
6	6	12	18	24	30	36	42	48	54	60	66	72
7	7	14	21	28	35	42	49	56	63	70	77	84
8	8	16	24	32	40	48	56	64	72	80	88	96
9	9	18	27	36	45	54	63	72	81	90	99	108
10	10	20	30	40	50	60	70	80	90	100	110	120
11	11	22	33	44	55	66	77	88	99	110	121	132
12	12	24	36	48	60	72	84	96	108	120	132	144

DIVISION

Division is the opposite of multiplication; with division, you are splitting a number into equal parts. As such, memorizing the multiplication tables will help with quick division. For example, knowing that 12 × 8 = 96 makes it simple to find the answer to 96 ÷ 12. Because you know that 12 × 8 = 96, you know that the answer to 96 ÷ 12 is 8.

As we have seen with addition, subtraction, and multiplication, the simple problems are just that. You can probably figure them out easily enough. It is when you are faced with the larger numbers that require a bit of long division that you may get tripped up.

Long division appears scary to many people, and if you are one of them, you can feel confident that with a little review you can handle even the most complex division. Here is an example to work through: 5,952 divided by 32.

Start by writing out the problem in long form, to show that you are dividing 32 into 5,952.

MEMO
RE: DIVISION TERMS
The number being divided is called the *dividend*, and the number doing the dividing is the *divisor*. The result of the division is called the *quotient*. For example, in 15 ÷ 5 = 3, 15 is the dividend, 5 is the divisor, and 3 is the quotient.

$$32\overline{)5952}$$

Because you can't divide 32 into the first digit, because 5 is less than 32, divide 32 into 59. It goes in 1 time, so write that on top of the line above the 9 and put 32 (essentially, 32 × 1) under the 59. The 1 is written above the 9 in the "59" because you just divided 32 into 59.

$$\begin{array}{r} 1 \\ 32\overline{)5952} \\ -32 \end{array}$$

Now, subtract 32 from 59 to get the remainder of 27.

$$\begin{array}{r} 1 \\ 32\overline{)5952} \\ \underline{-32} \\ 27 \end{array}$$

This number is less than 32, so bring the 5 down to make a number that is divisible by 32:

$$\begin{array}{r} 1 \\ 32\overline{)5952} \\ \underline{-32} \\ 275 \end{array}$$

Now, divide 275 by 32 and write the result, which is 8, on top.

$$\begin{array}{r} 18 \\ 32\overline{)5952} \\ \underline{-32} \\ 275 \\ \underline{256} \end{array}$$

Subtract 256 from 275 to get the remainder of 19:

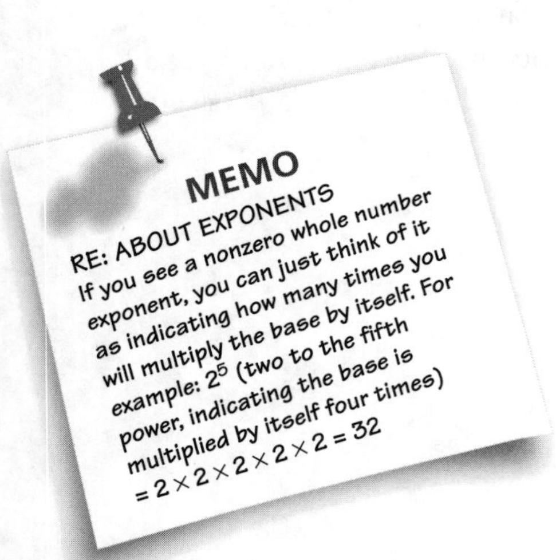

$$\begin{array}{r} 18 \\ 32\overline{)5952} \\ \underline{-32} \\ 275 \\ \underline{-256} \\ 19 \end{array}$$

Bring down the next number in the dividend, the 2:

$$\begin{array}{r} 18 \\ 32\overline{)5952} \\ \underline{-32} \\ 275 \\ \underline{-256} \\ 192 \end{array}$$

Divide the result by 32 and write the answer on top:

```
     186
32)5952
   -32
    275
   -256
    192
   -192
      0
```

The remainder at this point is 0, which means the problem has been solved. We have found that 5,952 divided by 32 is 186.

It's not as difficult as you remember, is it?

While division may never become your favorite process, being able to divide numbers accurately is important in business. You should be able to write out a division problem and solve it if a calculator is not available. That way, if you are in the middle of a meeting and you don't have a calculator with you, you won't be hamstrung if you are faced with a division problem.

MEMO

RE: NUMBER NAMES

Impress your coworkers with your knowledge of big numbers! Sure, most people know what a trillion is, but how many know what a vigintillion is? (It is a 1 followed by 63 zeros.) Here are the names of some large numbers:

10^1	ten	10^{33}	decillion
10^2	hundred	10^{36}	undecillion
10^3	thousand	10^{39}	duodecillion
10^6	million	10^{42}	tredecillion
10^9	billion	10^{45}	quattuordecillion
10^{12}	trillion	10^{48}	quindecillion
10^{15}	quadrillion	10^{51}	sexdecillion
10^{18}	quintillion	10^{54}	septendecillion
10^{21}	sextillion	10^{57}	octodecillion
10^{24}	septillion	10^{60}	novemdecillion
10^{27}	octillion	10^{63}	vigintillion
10^{30}	nonillion		

ROMAN NUMERALS

Roman numerals are not used for common arithmetic or in most day-to-day commerce—probably a good thing considering they often appear as just a mishmash of letters to many people! They are still often used for outlines and presentations, however. For this reason, you should be able to recognize them and understand the convention for writing Roman numerals of different values.

All Roman numerals are written using a combination of seven letters representing numeric values:

I = 1
V = 5
X = 10
L = 50
C = 100
D = 500
M = 1,000

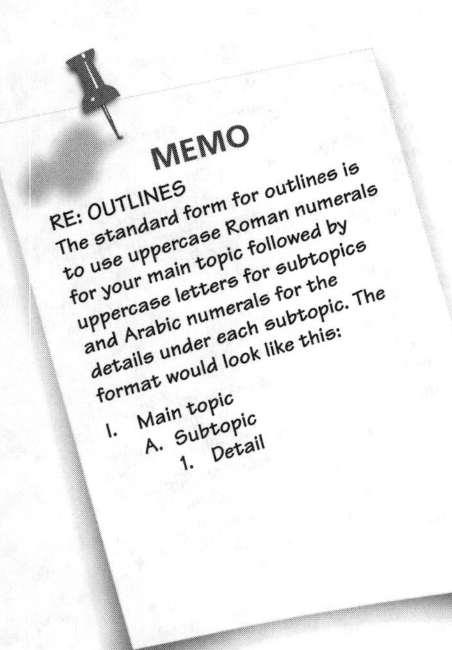

One key to understanding Roman numerals is the placement of the large versus small numerals in a combination. If a smaller number follows a larger one, the numbers are added together:

VII: 5 + 1 + 1 = 7
LX: 50 + 10 = 60
MDVI: 1,000 + 500 + 5 + 1 = 1,506

If a smaller number *precedes* a larger one, then the smaller number is subtracted from the larger one:

IV: 5 – 1 = 4
XC: 100 – 10 = 90
CDXL: (500 – 100) + (50 – 10) = 400 + 40 = 440

Another key to Roman numerals is that a letter can be repeated only three times when expressing a number. For example, you would write CCC for 300, but you wouldn't write CCCC for 400. You would express 400 as CD (500 – 100). Roman numerals can be written as lowercase or uppercase letters without changing their numeric value.

ROMAN NUMERALS TABLE

1	I	**11**	XI	**21**	XXI	**90**	XC	**600**	DC
2	II	**12**	XII	**30**	XXX	**100**	C	**700**	DCC
3	III	**13**	XIII	**31**	XXXI	**101**	CI	**800**	DCCC
4	IV	**14**	XIV	**40**	XL	**150**	CL	**900**	CM
5	V	**15**	XV	**41**	XLI	**151**	CLI	**1,000**	M
6	VI	**16**	XVI	**50**	L	**200**	CC	**1,001**	MI
7	VII	**17**	XVII	**51**	LI	**201**	CCI	**1,500**	MD
8	VIII	**18**	XVIII	**60**	LX	**300**	CCC	**1,600**	MDC
9	IX	**19**	XIX	**70**	LXX	**400**	CD	**2,000**	MM
10	X	**20**	XX	**80**	LXXX	**500**	D	**2,001**	MMI

PRACTICE QUIZ

1. 60 + 89 =
2. 126 + 38 =
3. 539 + 348 =
4. 866 + 229 =
5. 17,776 + 7,432 =
6. 38,967 + 12,453 =
7. 55,188 + 27,339 =
8. At the monthly production meeting, the warehouse manager reported that the following drop shipments had been received: 3,421 red units, 674 blue units, 1,801 green units, and 5,732 yellow units. How many total units were received?
9. 128 – 13 =
10. 140 – 29 =
11. 667 – 73 =
12. 12,892 – 13 =
13. 21,300 – 12,299 =
14. 81,562 – 9,341 =
15. 9 × 7 =
16. 12 × 12 =
17. 18 × 4 =
18. 86 × 21 =
19. 371 × 49 =
20. 14,820 × 27 =
21. 23,892 × 50 =
22. 567 × 15,637 =
23. Annie receives a paycheck twice a month. Her take-home pay in each semi-monthly paycheck is $1,605. What is her yearly take-home pay?
24. 28 ÷ 14 =
25. 55 ÷ 11 =
26. 426 ÷ 6 =
27. 16,498 ÷ 4 =
28. 32,335 ÷ 25 =
29. 8,722 ÷ 80 =
30. A company has 14 departments, all sharing equally the cost of new servers. The total cost for the servers is $48,628. What is each department's share?

Convert the following Roman numerals to Arabic numerals:

31. XVIII
32. CCXCV
33. MXCII

CHAPTER TWO

Fractions and Decimals

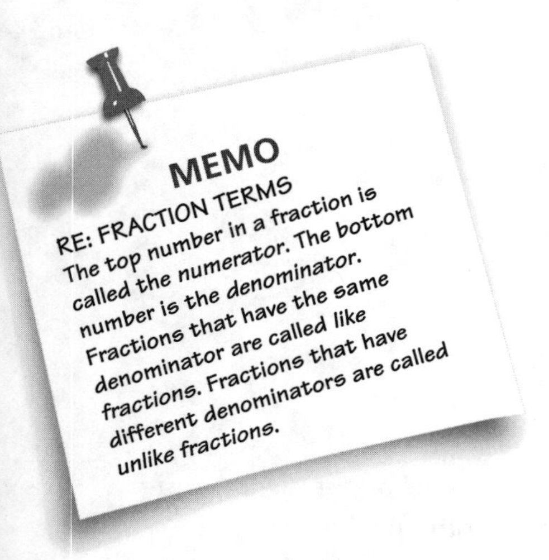

Fractions are special numbers that describe a part of a whole. They show the relationship between a part and its whole. Decimal numbers accomplish the same thing, only in a different format. You will undoubtedly run into fractions and decimals in your daily job, so understanding how to work with them is very important to your success. This chapter reviews the basic concepts related to fractions and decimals and shows you how to convert from one to the other.

ADDING FRACTIONS

There are three steps to adding fractions:

1. Make sure the denominators are the same. If they are not, find a common denominator for the fractions that you want to add together.
2. Add the numerators and place the result on top of the denominator. *Do not add the denominators!*
3. Simplify the fraction, if necessary.

Here is an example of adding fractions that have the same denominator:

$$\frac{7}{15}+\frac{3}{15}$$

You can skip step 1, because the denominators are the same. Moving on to step 2, add the numerators and place the sum on top of the denominator:

$$\frac{7}{15}+\frac{3}{15}=\frac{10}{15}$$

Now, simplify the fraction. What is the largest number by which both the numerator and the denominator can be divided? When you are looking for numbers that your number can be divided by (without any remainders), you are looking for *factors*. To think about factors in your head for the number 10, think: *One times ten, two times five, and that's it!* So, looking at the factors of 10, we have: 1, 2, 5, and 10. To think about factors in your head for the number 15, think: *One times fifteen, three times five, and that's it!* So, looking at the factors of 15, we have: 1, 3, 5, 15. The largest number by which both the numerator and the denominator can be divided is 5. This is the greatest common factor. To simplify the fraction, divide the numerator and the denominator by the greatest common factor:

MEMO

RE: SIMPLIFYING FRACTIONS

To simplify a fraction to the lowest terms, you have to change it into an equivalent fraction where the numerator and the denominator are as small as possible. When a fraction is correctly simplified, no number, other than 1, can be divided evenly into both the numerator and the denominator.

After finding the greatest common factor, which is the largest factor that can be divided evenly into both the numerator and the denominator, divide the numerator and the denominator by it. The result is your simplified fraction.

$$\frac{10 \div 5}{15 \div 5}=\frac{2}{3}$$

The simplified fraction becomes $\frac{2}{3}$ because $10 \div 5 = 2$, and $15 \div 5 = 3$.

When the denominators are not the same, you will have an extra step. Let's look at this problem:

$$\frac{2}{6}+\frac{4}{15}$$

Here, you need to find the least common denominator (the smallest number that is a multiple of both denominators). Start by looking at the larger denominator.

Can it be divided by the smaller one? In this case, no, 15 cannot be evenly divided by 6. So, move on to the next multiple of 15, which is 30. Can 30 be divided evenly by 6? Yes, so 30 is the least common denominator for the two fractions.

You must multiply the numerators by the same number by which you will multiply the denominators. The first fraction looks like this:

$$\frac{2\times 5}{6\times 5}=\frac{10}{30}$$

The new fraction becomes $\frac{10}{30}$. Here is the second fraction:

$$\frac{4\times 2}{15\times 2}=\frac{8}{30}$$

The new fraction becomes $\frac{8}{30}$. Now you can add the two fractions:

$$\frac{10}{30}+\frac{8}{30}=\frac{18}{30}$$

Remember the final step? *Simplify the fraction.* Divide the numerator and the denominator by the greatest common factor. In this case, the greatest common factor is 6:

$$\frac{18\div 6}{30\div 6}=\frac{3}{5}$$

The answer to $\frac{2}{6}+\frac{4}{15}$ is $\frac{3}{5}$.

SUBTRACTING FRACTIONS

The process for subtracting fractions is similar to the one for adding fractions:

1. Make sure the denominators are the same. If they are not, find a common denominator for the fractions.
2. Subtract the second numerator from the first and place the result on top of the denominator. *Do not subtract the denominators!*
3. Simplify the fraction, if necessary.

Here is an example:

$$\frac{4}{3} - \frac{2}{5}$$

The denominators are not the same, so your first step is to find the least common denominator. In this example, it is 15. Multiply the numerators and the denominators of each fraction by the same number to get to the least common denominator:

$$\frac{4 \times 5}{3 \times 5} = \frac{20}{15}$$

The first fraction becomes $\frac{20}{15}$. The next fraction in the problem looks like this:

$$\frac{2 \times 3}{5 \times 3} = \frac{6}{15}$$

The second fraction becomes $\frac{6}{15}$.

Now that the fractions have the same denominator, you can finish the problem.

$$\frac{20}{15} - \frac{6}{15} = \frac{14}{15}$$

This fraction cannot to be simplified any further, so the result of $\frac{4}{3} - \frac{2}{5}$ is $\frac{14}{15}$.

MEMO

RE: RATIOS

Ratios are used to make comparisons between two things. They can be written either separated by a slash (virgule), by using words, or by using a colon. For example, if there are ten programmers and three account managers in the office, the ratio of programmers to account managers can be written:

- with a slash: 10/3
- using words: ten to three
- with a colon: 10:3

MULTIPLYING FRACTIONS

Multiplying fractions only seems difficult. Follow these steps to multiply fractions simply and correctly:

1. Multiply the numerators. The product is your new numerator.
2. Multiply the denominators. The product is your new denominator.
3. Simplify the fraction, if necessary.

Let's work through a sample problem:

$$\frac{3}{4} \times \frac{6}{7}$$

Multiply the numerators:

$$3 \times 6 = 18$$

Multiply the denominators:

$$4 \times 7 = 28$$

Write the products in fraction form:

$$\frac{18}{28}$$

This fraction can be simplified, so find the greatest common factor and divide both the numerator and the denominator by that number. In this example, the greatest common factor is 2:

$$\frac{18 \div 2}{28 \div 2} = \frac{9}{14}$$

MEMO
RE: MIXED FRACTIONS
A mixed fraction is a whole number combined with a fraction, such as $2\frac{3}{4}$. You can always express a mixed fraction as just one fraction by turning the whole number into a fraction and adding it to the existing fraction. In the case of $2\frac{3}{4}$, 2 would become $\frac{8}{4}$ (the equivalent fraction). Then you would add $\frac{8}{4}$ to $\frac{3}{4}$ to get your new fraction: $\frac{11}{4}$. This is called an improper fraction because the numerator is larger than the denominator.

The answer to $\frac{3}{4} \times \frac{6}{7}$ is $\frac{9}{14}$.

DIVIDING FRACTIONS

If dividing fractions seems a little trickier than the other operations we have reviewed, don't worry—it isn't! To divide fractions, you follow the steps for multiplying fractions—although there is one additional key step at the beginning of the process.

The key to dividing fractions is to turn the second fraction, the one you are dividing by (the divisor), into its reciprocal. Essentially, you are flipping the numerator and the denominator.

Reciprocal examples:

Fraction	*Reciprocal*
$\frac{1}{2}$	$\frac{2}{1}$
$\frac{4}{5}$	$\frac{5}{4}$
$\frac{16}{25}$	$\frac{25}{16}$
$2\frac{2}{5}$	First convert $2\frac{2}{5}$ to the improper fraction $\frac{12}{5}$, and then flip to get $\frac{5}{12}$.

Once you have turned the divisor into a reciprocal, follow the steps for multiplying fractions: Multiply the numerators, multiply the denominators, and simplify the resulting fraction (if necessary).

Here is an example of how to divide fractions using $\frac{1}{6} \div \frac{1}{4}$.

First, turn the second fraction into a reciprocal: $\frac{1}{4}$ becomes $\frac{4}{1}$.

Now the division problem becomes a multiplication problem. Set it up so you are multiplying the first fraction by the reciprocal of the second:

$$\frac{1}{6} \times \frac{4}{1}$$

Multiply the numerators:

$$1 \times 4 = 4$$

Then multiply the denominators:

$$6 \times 1 = 6$$

The new fraction is now $\frac{4}{6}$. The last step is to simplify the fraction. Both the numerator and the denominator can be divided by 2 to create the final answer: $\frac{2}{3}$.

CONVERTING FRACTIONS TO DECIMALS

You have two options when converting fractions to decimals: You can use multiplication, or you can divide the numerator by the denominator.

The multiplication option requires you to follow these three steps:

1. If the denominator is not 10, 100, or any other power of 10, make it so by finding a number by which you can multiply both the numerator and the

denominator so that the denominator becomes 10, 100, or another power of 10.
2. Multiply the numerator and denominator by the number.
3. Take the new numerator and put the decimal place in the correct position. It should be placed one space from the left of its starting position for every zero in the denominator. Essentially, you are dividing the new numerator by the new denominator. The result is your equivalent decimal number.

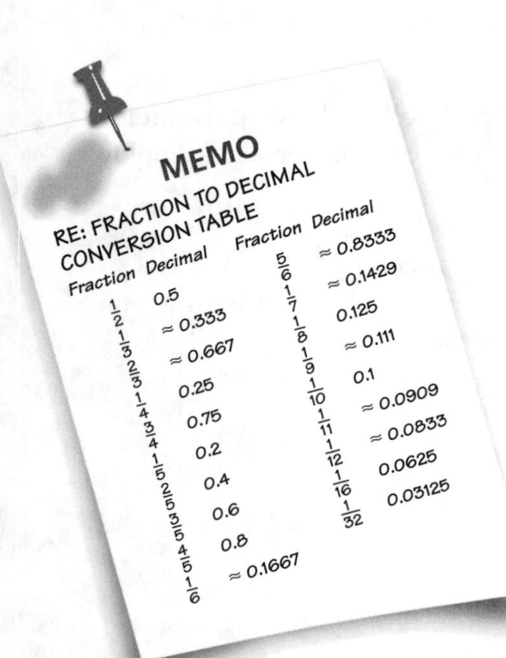
MEMO

RE: FRACTION TO DECIMAL CONVERSION TABLE

Fraction	Decimal	Fraction	Decimal
$\frac{1}{2}$	0.5	$\frac{5}{6}$	≈ 0.8333
$\frac{1}{3}$	≈ 0.333	$\frac{1}{7}$	≈ 0.1429
$\frac{2}{3}$	≈ 0.667	$\frac{1}{8}$	0.125
$\frac{1}{4}$	0.25	$\frac{1}{9}$	≈ 0.111
$\frac{3}{4}$	0.75	$\frac{1}{10}$	0.1
$\frac{1}{5}$	0.2	$\frac{1}{11}$	≈ 0.0909
$\frac{2}{5}$	0.4	$\frac{1}{12}$	≈ 0.0833
$\frac{3}{5}$	0.6	$\frac{1}{16}$	0.0625
$\frac{4}{5}$	0.8	$\frac{1}{32}$	0.03125
$\frac{1}{6}$	≈ 0.1667		

Here is an example of how to convert a fraction to a decimal using the multiplication option:

Start with the fraction $\frac{5}{8}$. The lowest number that the denominator can become is 1,000 (8 × 125 = 1,000). Multiply the numerator and the denominator by 125:

$$\frac{5 \times 125}{8 \times 125} = \frac{625}{1{,}000}$$

The new fraction is $\frac{625}{1{,}000}$ and can be converted into a decimal number by simply moving the decimal point of the numerator three places from the right to yield 0.625.

Thus, $\frac{5}{8} = 0.625$.

CONVERTING DECIMALS TO FRACTIONS

Just as with converting fractions to decimals, there are three steps to follow to convert decimals to fractions:

1. Multiply the decimal number by a power of 10 (10, 100, etc.) to move the decimal point all the way to the right.
2. Make the result your numerator and place it on top of the number by which you multiplied in step 1, your new denominator.
3. Simplify the fraction, if necessary.

Let's work through those three steps using 0.6. The decimal point needs to be moved only one place to the right, so multiply it by 10 (step 1) and create your new fraction (step 2):

$$\frac{6}{10}$$

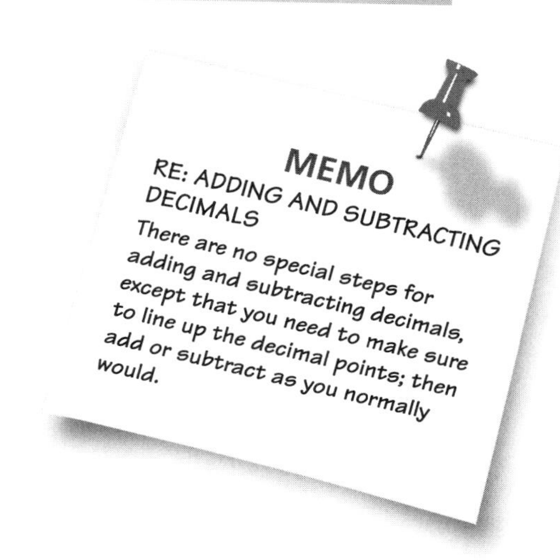

Now, simplify the fraction by dividing the numerator and the denominator by 2 (step 3):

$$\frac{6 \div 2}{10 \div 2} = \frac{3}{5}$$

The new fraction is $\frac{3}{5}$. So, $0.6 = \frac{3}{5}$.

MULTIPLYING DECIMALS

Multiplying decimals is not that much different from multiplying whole numbers. The primary difference is that you need to remember to properly place the decimal point after you have finished multiplying the numbers.

To multiply decimal numbers, align them on the right, as you would whole numbers. Do not align the decimal points.

$$\begin{array}{r} 14.66 \\ \times\ 1.2 \\ \hline \end{array}$$

Then, follow the rules for multiplying whole numbers, ignoring the decimal points while you do so. Start on the right and multiply each digit in the top number by each digit in the bottom number. Then, add the products together.

$$\begin{array}{r} 14.66 \\ \times\ 1.2 \\ \hline 2932 \\ +\ 14660 \\ \hline 17592 \end{array}$$

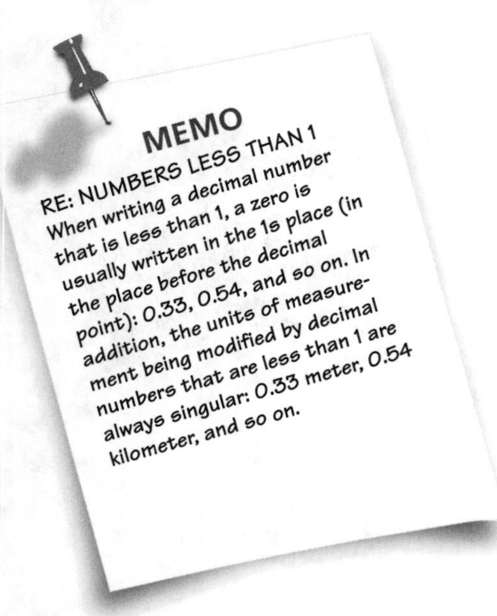

Now that you have completed multiplying the two numbers, you need to place the decimal point correctly. To do so, count the number of decimal places in each multiplier and add them together. In our example, the first number is expressed to the hundredth place (there are two decimal places), and the second number is expressed to the tenths place (one decimal place), for a total of three decimal places. To place the decimal point in our answer, start at the right and count over three decimal places so the final answer becomes 17.592.

DIVIDING DECIMALS

Dividing decimals is similar to dividing whole numbers. The only extra step to take is to place the decimal point properly. When you are dividing a decimal number by a whole number, start by placing a decimal point in the quotient directly above the one in the dividend. You would write 7.2 ÷ 4 like this:

$$\begin{array}{r} . \\ 4\overline{)7.2} \end{array}$$

Divide 4 into 7 to get 1, with 3 remaining.

$$\begin{array}{r} 1. \\ 4\overline{)7.2} \\ \underline{-4} \\ 3 \end{array}$$

Bring down the 2 and divide 4 into 32 to get 8:

$$\begin{array}{r} 1.8 \\ 4\overline{)7.2} \\ \underline{-4} \\ 3\,2 \\ \underline{-3\,2} \\ 0 \end{array}$$

There is nothing remaining, so the answer to $7.2 \div 4$ is 1.8.

Dividing a decimal number into another decimal number or even into a whole number requires one additional step. You must make the divisor a whole number. To do that, move the decimal points of both the divisor and the dividend to the right an equal number of places so that the divisor becomes whole. Then, you follow the steps as before. Let's take $6.075 \div 0.081$ as an example.

Your first step is to convert 0.081 to a whole number. To do that, move the decimal point three places to the right. You will also need to move the decimal three places to the right in the dividend.

0.081 becomes 81
6.075 becomes 6075

Now, set up the division problem as you would with whole numbers:

$$81\overline{)6075}$$

Divide 607 by 81, which is 7 with 40 remaining:

$$\begin{array}{r} 7 \\ 81\overline{)6075} \\ -\underline{567} \\ 40 \end{array}$$

Bring down the 5 and divide 405 by 81 to get 5:

$$\begin{array}{r} 75 \\ 81\overline{)6075} \\ -\underline{567} \\ 405 \\ -\underline{405} \\ 0 \end{array}$$

There is nothing remaining, so the answer to $6.075 \div 0.081$ is 75.

PRACTICE QUIZ

1. $\frac{3}{8} + \frac{5}{12} =$
2. $\frac{5}{6} + \frac{4}{6} =$
3. $1\frac{1}{2} + \frac{1}{4} =$
4. $\frac{3}{4} - \frac{1}{2} =$
5. $\frac{4}{9} - \frac{13}{72} =$
6. $\frac{5}{8} - \frac{9}{16} =$
7. $10.34 \times 9.2 =$
8. $142.3 \times 3 =$
9. $127 \times 0.548 =$
10. $348.52 \div 2 =$
11. $29 \div 0.33 =$
12. $2.470 \div 0.095 =$

Convert the following fractions to decimals:
13. $\frac{3}{5}$
14. $\frac{2}{7}$
15. $\frac{7}{8}$
16. $\frac{8}{35}$

Convert the following decimals to fractions:
17. 0.3
18. 0.015
19. 0.25
20. 0.65

CHAPTER THREE

Basic Measurements

Measurement is a basic skill that is important regardless of profession. At some point in your career, you will run into a situation where you must measure something—a package for shipping, for example—or you will have to read and understand materials that include measurements. For some professionals, including designers, engineers, and scientists, measurements are critical to their daily work.

Measurements are generally expressed in either metric or U.S. Conventional System of Measurement units (which we refer to as U.S. units in this chapter). You are probably most familiar with U.S. units, the pounds and inches type of measurements. But understanding metric units of measurement is important in an increasingly global economy. Having a working knowledge of the metric system will give you an edge as you progress in your career.

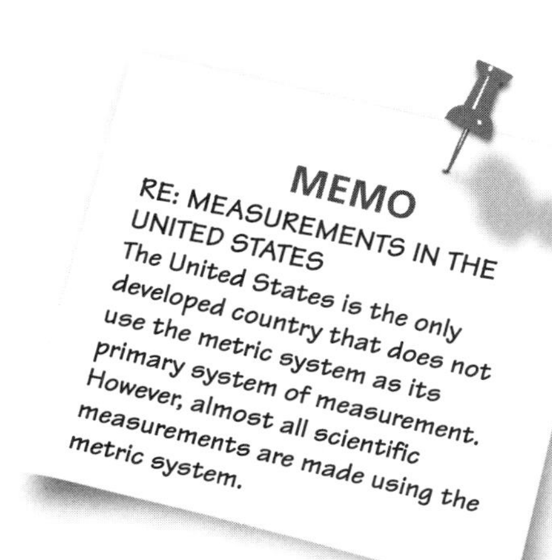

This chapter will provide you with a review of basic measurements in U.S. and metric units. It will also show how to convert U.S. units to metric units and vice versa.

U.S. UNITS

U.S. units are the pounds and inches measurements. They are the measurements we use in our day-to-day lives, those found in cookbooks, at gas stations, and on car dashboards, for example. These units are based on the human body. An inch, for example,

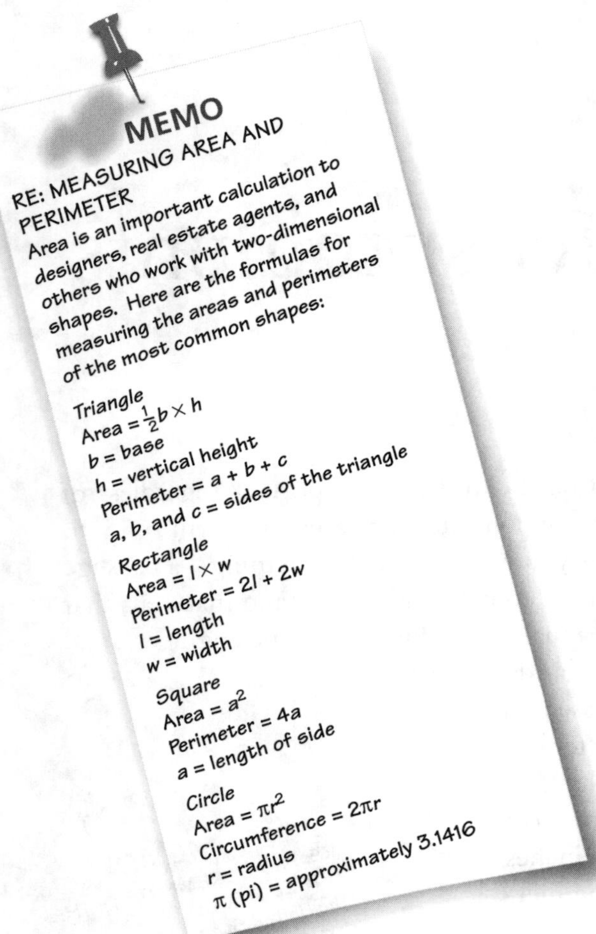

was originally defined as being equal to the width of a person's thumb—in French, *pouce* means both "thumb" and "inch." This common meaning occurs in other languages as well.

Some of the U.S. units we know may be based on parts of the body, but now we know them based on their relationships with each other and on various measuring tools. Here are the most common U.S. units and how they relate:

1 foot (ft.) = 12 inches (in.)
1 yard (yd.) = 3 feet = 36 inches
1 mile (mi.) = 1,760 yards = 5,280 feet
1 acre = 43,560 square feet

1 teaspoon (tsp.) = $\frac{1}{6}$ fluid ounce (fl. oz.)
1 tablespoon (tbsp.) = $\frac{1}{2}$ fluid ounce
1 cup (c.) = 8 fluid ounces
1 pint (pt.) = 2 cups
1 quart (qt.) = 2 pints = 4 cups
1 gallon (gal.) = 4 quarts

1 pound (lb.) = 16 ounces (oz.)
1 ton (T.) = 2,000 pounds

METRIC MEASUREMENTS

The metric system has existed for more than 300 years. It uses seven base units along with prefixes to represent its units of measurement. The seven base units are:

1. *meter* to measure length
2. *gram* to measure mass
3. *second* to measure time
4. *ampere* to measure electric currents
5. *Kelvin* and *degrees Celsius* to measure temperature
6. *mole* to measure the amount of substance
7. *candela* to measure luminous intensity

METRIC SYMBOLS

It is important to use metric symbols properly. There are three key points to remember regarding usage. First, the symbols are case-sensitive, and uppercase and lowercase letters have different meanings. A lowercase *m* means *milli*, but an uppercase *M* means *mega*—signifying very different amounts! Second, there are neither singular nor plural forms of the symbols, so there is never an "s" at the end of a symbol even if more than one unit is being expressed. You would write 1 cm and 13 cm, never 13 cms. Finally, because they are symbols, not abbreviations, they do not require a period.

The following tables show the most common metric symbols:

Length, Width, Distance, Thickness

millimeter	mm
centimeter	cm
meter	m
kilometer	km

Weight

milligram	mg
gram	g
kilogram	kg
metric ton (tonne)	t

Area

square meter	m^2
hectare	ha
square kilometer	km^2

Volume

milliliter	mL
cubic centimeter	cm^3
liter	L
cubic meter	m^3

Speed

meter per second	m/s
kilometer per hour	km/h

Power

watt	W
kilowatt	kW

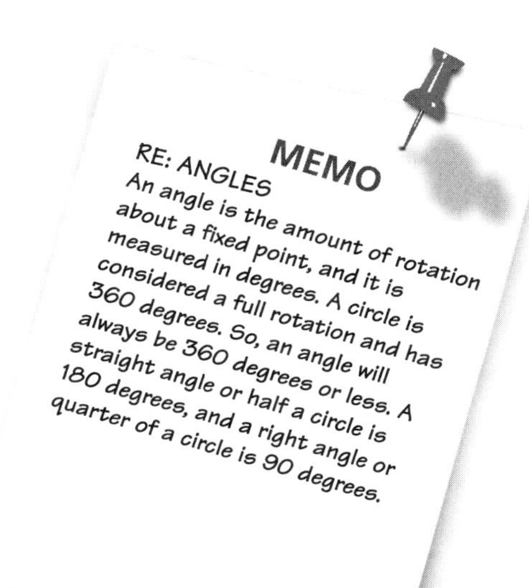

CONVERTING FROM ONE SYSTEM TO THE OTHER

To convert from metric units to U.S. units and vice versa, you must know the correct conversion number. Chances are you aren't going to commit all of the conversion numbers to memory, but you might try to remember a few of them. Your best option is to create a chart that you can refer to whenever you need to convert from one system of measurement to the other.

Let's look at an example of how to convert U.S. units to metric units:

Say you have an item that you need to ship, and it weighs 8.5 pounds. Your shipping cost chart, however, lists the costs in kilograms, so you need to convert 8.5 pounds to kilograms. To do so, you would find the conversion number for pounds to kilograms:

1 pound = 0.4536 kilograms

Then, multiply the number of pounds by the conversion number:

$$8.5 \times 0.4536$$

The answer is 3.8556. For the purpose of this example, you would then round the amount up to 4 kilograms and find the corresponding shipping charge.

The following two tables show the conversion numbers that you should use to convert the systems of measurement.

Metric Units to U.S. Units Conversion Tables

Values are approximated where appropriate.

Length	
1 millimeter	0.03937 inch
1 centimeter	0.3937 inch
1 meter	1.0936 yards
1 kilometer	0.6214 mile
Area	
1 square centimeter	0.1550 square inch
1 square meter	1.1960 square yards
1 hectare	2.4711 acres
1 square kilometer	0.3861 square mile
Volume	
1 cubic centimeter	0.0610 cubic inch
1 cubic decimeter	0.0353 cubic foot
1 cubic meter	1.3080 cubic yards
1 liter	1.76 pints
1 hectoliter	21.997 gallons

Mass

1 gram	0.0353 ounce
1 kilogram	2.2046 pounds
1 tonne (metric ton)	0.9842 ton

U.S. Units to Metric Units Conversion Tables

Values are approximated where appropriate.

Length

1 inch	2.54 centimeters
1 foot	0.3048 meter
1 yard	0.9144 meter
1 mile	1.6093 kilometers

Area

1 square inch	6.4516 square cm
1 square foot	0.0929 square m
1 square yard	0.8361 square m
1 acre	4,046.9 square m
1 square mile	2.59 square km

Volume

1 fluid ounce	29.574 milliliters
1 pint	0.4731 liter
1 gallon	3.7854 liters

Mass

1 ounce	28.35 grams
1 pound	0.4536 kilogram

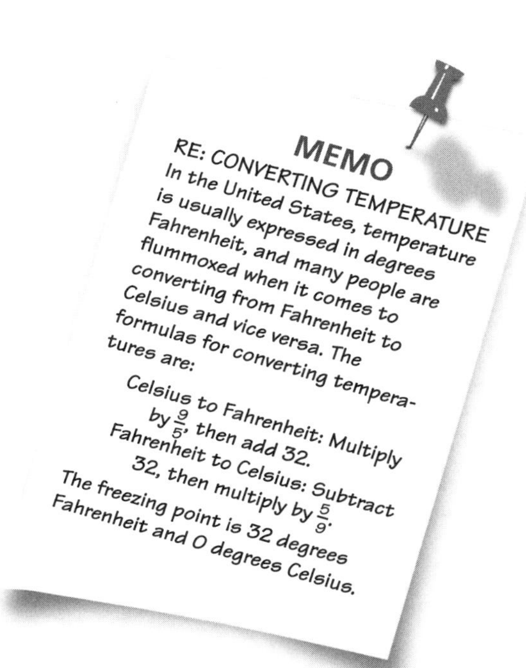

PRACTICE QUIZ

1. How many inches are in 16 feet?
2. Convert 60 degrees Celsius to Fahrenheit.
3. Forty-eight feet is equal to how many yards?
4. How many feet are in three miles?
5. Convert 95 degrees Fahrenheit to Celsius.
6. Convert 300 millimeters to inches.
7. Convert five miles to kilometers.
8. How many feet are in 2.5 yards?

9. How many ounces are in 6.5 pounds?
10. Convert 70 degrees Fahrenheit to Celsius.
11. Convert 15 degrees Celsius to Fahrenheit.
12. What is the area of a square that has 11-inch sides?
13. How many liters are in five pints?
14. What is the area of a triangle with a base of 10 inches and a height of 7 inches?

CHAPTER FOUR

Percentages

Percentages are involved in many daily decisions and activities—within the business world and without. Sales taxes, discounts, and poll results, for example, are all commonly stated in percentages. Understanding how percentages work will allow you to comprehend more of the information that you encounter, from survey results and interest rates to manufacturing data and sales figures. This chapter explains what percentages are and how to work with them.

PRINCIPLES OF PERCENTAGES

The word *percent* means "per hundred." When you see the percent symbol or the word *percent*, you can think of this as meaning "out of 100." So, when you talk about percentages, you are really talking about fractions where the denominator is 100. For example, 25% is 25 out of 100, or $\frac{25}{100}$, which can be simplified to $\frac{1}{4}$.

Use the following formula to find what percentage a particular number is of another:

$$\frac{\%}{100} = \frac{\text{is}}{\text{of}}$$

The way to use this formula is to think "Percent over 100 equals 'is' over 'of.'" So if you want to determine what percentage 13 is of 70, you would set up the equation like this:

$$\frac{x}{100} = \frac{13}{70}$$

This means x (percent, the unknown) over 100 equals 13 (the "is") over 70 (the "of").

To finish the equation, you would cross multiply:

$$70x = 1{,}300$$

Then, divide both sides by 70 to find x, the percent:

$$x = 18.57 \text{ (when rounded to the nearest hundredth)}$$

The answer: 13 is 18.57% of 70.

Let's take another example. Say you know that a salesperson was responsible for 15% of the total sales for a particular quarter. If the total sales were 6,500 units, how many did that salesperson sell?

Here, you know the percentage, so you would place that over 100:

$$\frac{15}{100}$$

You don't know the "is" in this problem, so that would become x, your unknown. You do know the "of," which is the total sales or 6,500 units. Your equation would look like this:

$$\frac{15}{100} = \frac{x}{6{,}500}$$

If you cross multiply, you get:

$$100x = 97{,}500$$

Now, divide each side by 100 to solve for x:

$$x = 975$$

If the salesperson made 15% of the total sales, then she sold 975 units.

Here's an example using sales tax. If you want to buy an item that costs $298 and the tax rate is 8%, how much will you have to pay? We'll plug the numbers into our formula to figure this out:

$$\frac{8}{10} = \frac{x}{298}$$

Cross multiply:

$$100x = 2{,}384$$

Divide each side by 100:

$$x = 23.84$$

The sales tax that you would have to pay would be $23.84. Your total cost would be the price of the item, $298, plus the tax, $23.84, or $321.84.

CONVERTING FRACTIONS TO PERCENTAGES AND VICE VERSA

To convert a fraction to a percentage, divide the numerator by the denominator. Then move the decimal point two places to the right (i.e., multiply by 100) and add a percent sign.

If you want to express $\frac{3}{8}$ as a percentage, divide 3 by 8 to get 0.375. Then move the decimal point two places to the right (37.5) and add a percent sign. Now you know that $\frac{3}{8}$ is equal to 37.5%.

How about $\frac{19}{50}$?

Just divide 50 into 19 to get 0.38. Move the decimal point two places to the right and add the percent sign: 38%.

To convert a percentage to a fraction, place the percentage amount over 100 to set up your fraction. Then, simplify the fraction if possible.

If the percentage is not a whole number (if, for example, you wish to convert a percentage such as 5.5%), then multiply the numerator (your original percentage) and the denominator (100) by 10 for every number after the decimal point. This sounds more difficult than it is. Let's look at an example:

To convert 22.75% to a fraction, first place the percentage amount over 100:

$$\frac{22.75}{100}$$

Because the percentage is not a whole number, you must multiply the numerator and denominator by 10 for each number after the decimal point. In this example, there are two numbers after the decimal point, so you would multiply by 10 twice, which is the same as multiplying by 100:

$$\frac{22.75 \times 100}{100 \times 100} = \frac{2{,}275}{10{,}000}$$

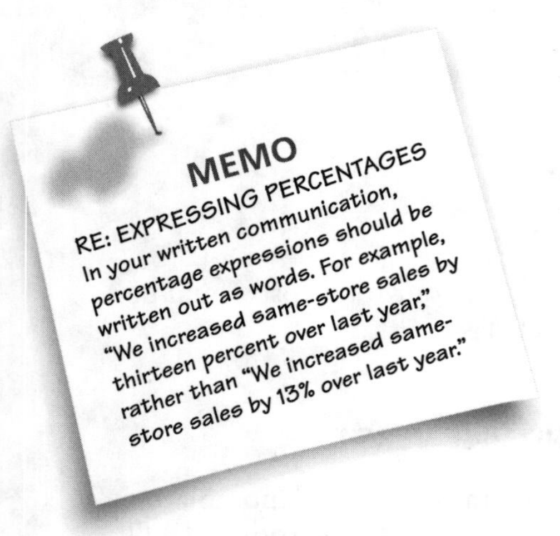

The new fraction, $\frac{2,275}{10,000}$, is pretty large, isn't it? This can be simplified by dividing the numerator and the denominator by the greatest common factor. In our example, the greatest common factor is 25:

$$\frac{2,275 \div 25}{10,000 \div 25} = \frac{91}{400}$$

The fraction becomes $\frac{91}{400}$. So, 22.75% is equal to $\frac{91}{400}$.

PERCENTAGE DIFFERENCE

Percentage difference shows the difference between two numbers as a percentage of the larger value. To figure out the percentage difference, first calculate the difference by subtracting one number from the other. Then, divide the difference by the larger value. Finish by converting the result to a percentage by multiplying it by 100. The formula for percentage difference is:

$$\text{percentage difference} = (\text{difference} \div \text{larger value}) \times 100$$

Here is an example:

An office manager is comparing total billable hours for two weeks. The total billable hours for week one is 250, and the total for week two is 210. What is the percentage of fewer hours billed in week two?

To figure this out, first find the difference in the total amounts billed in the two weeks.

$$250 - 210 = 40$$

Now, plug this into the formula to calculate the percentage difference:

$$(40 \div 250) \times 100 = 0.16 \times 100 = 16\%$$

The percentage difference between total billable hours for weeks one and two is 16%. The office billed 16% fewer hours in week two.

PERCENTAGE INCREASE OR DECREASE

Let's look at a percentage increase. If your salary is \$52,000 per year and you are offered a new job with a salary of \$56,000, what would the percentage increase be?

To find the percentage increase, find the difference in the two salaries.

$$\$56{,}000 - \$52{,}000 = \$4{,}000$$

MEMO

RE: PERCENTAGE INCREASES AND DECREASES

Percentage increases and decreases are calculated on the value that existed before the increase or decrease occurred. The formula for percentage increases and decreases is:

(difference ÷ old value) × 100

The percentage increase must be calculated on the original value, your current salary of \$52,000. So, you would divide \$4,000 by \$52,000 to get 0.077 (after rounding). To convert this to a percentage, complete the calculation by multiplying 0.077 by 100 to get 7.7%. At \$56,000 per year, you would realize a 7.7% increase in your salary with the new job.

REVERSING PERCENTAGE INCREASES AND DECREASES

A common mistake is thinking that a percentage increase can be reversed by applying the same percentage decrease (or vice versa). It cannot. For example, a 10% increase from 100 is 10, making the new amount 110. If you try to reverse the percentage increase by decreasing 110 by 10%, you will end up with 99 because 10% of 110 is 11. Clearly, 99 is not the same amount that you started with.

How, then, can percentage increases and decreases be reversed? By using the formulas listed here.

To reverse:

- a percentage increase (x = percentage increase): $x \div [1 + (x \div 100)]$
- a percentage decrease (y = percentage decrease): $y \div [1 - (y \div 100)]$

Using the example from before, to reverse a 10% increase, the equation would look like this:

$$10 \div [1 + (10 \div 100)] = 10 \div 1.1 = 9.091 \text{ (when rounded)}$$

Decreasing 110 by 9.091% brings you back to the original amount, 100.

PRACTICE QUIZ

1. What is 20% of 80?
2. Convert 83% to a decimal.
3. What is 38% of 50?
4. Calculate the amount of sales tax on an item that sells for $49.99 using a 7% tax rate.
5. What percentage is 7 of 63?
6. What percentage is 12 of 90?
7. Convert 0.125 to a percent.
8. If 350 people were asked to participate in a marketing survey and 260 of them actually completed the survey, what percentage of those asked went on to complete the survey?
9. Convert 35.75% to a fraction.
10. The suggested retail price for a product is $29.95. If a retailer purchases 52 units at a 40% discount, what is the total cost of the order?
11. Convert $\frac{5}{8}$ to a percent.
12. If you sold 316 units last quarter, how many units would you need to sell to realize a 15% increase this quarter?
13. Convert $\frac{9}{10}$ to a percent.
14. Calculate the return percentage: 435 units sold, 29 units returned.
15. Convert 5% to a fraction.

PART two

Business Applications

CHAPTER FIVE

Calculating Interest

There are two types of interest: simple and compound. These vary in the way that the interest is added to the principal. This chapter explains the difference between the two and how to calculate each.

SIMPLE INTEREST

Simple interest is calculated only on the original principal and is generally used for short periods, typically of less than a year. With simple interest, the amount of the deposit remains the same, because the interest is added at the end of a set period of time.

To calculate simple interest, you multiply the principal (the original dollar amount borrowed or lent) by the interest rate (per year) for one period and then by the total number of periods (in years). The result is added to the principal. You can remember how to calculate simple interest by thinking of it in terms of a formula:

$$\text{simple interest} = \text{principal} \times \text{rate} \times \text{time}$$

When calculating simple interest, pay attention to the period for which the interest rate is listed versus the total length of period for which interest will be calculated. As we've stated, simple interest is typically used for short periods. Thus, if an annual interest rate is quoted but the period is only three months, then the number of periods would be 0.25, because three months is one-quarter of a year.

Suppose you work for a start-up company that needs to take out a four-month loan of $8,000 to cover payroll because of a lag in accounts receivable.

The interest rate on the loan is 12%. How much would the company have to pay back? Just plug the numbers into the formula to figure this out:

$$\text{simple interest} = \$8{,}000 \times 0.12 \times 0.33$$

Notice that you have to write the interest rate and time period in decimal form. Because the loan is for four months, or one-third of a year, the time period is 0.33. Now, complete the calculation:

$$\text{simple interest} = \$316.80$$

The total amount that the company would pay back at the end of the loan period would be $8,316.80.

COMPOUND INTEREST

Compound interest is calculated on the original principal, plus the interest accumulated during past periods. The formula for compound interest is:

$$\text{compound interest} = \left[\text{principal} \times \left(1 + \frac{\text{rate}}{n}\right)^{\text{periods} \times n}\right] - \text{principal}$$

MEMO
RE: COMPOUNDING PERIODS
Interest can be compounded for any type of period: yearly, monthly, weekly, or daily, for example. When you are investing or taking out a loan, the financial institution should clearly state the compounding period for interest. If a lender charges 6% interest per year compounded monthly, you would be charged one-twelfth of that rate each month, or 0.5% per month.

In the formula, n represents the number of times the interest is compounded per year. Here's an example of calculating compound interest using a five-year loan of $6,000 at 4% compounded annually. Write out the interest rate as a decimal.

$$\text{compound interest} = [\$6{,}000 \times (1 + 0.04)^5] - \$6{,}000$$

Remember to use the correct order of operations! Start with the innermost parentheses:

$$1 + 0.04 = 1.04$$

Now, you can complete the multiplication. You will multiply $6,000 by 1.04 five times:

$$\$6{,}000 \times 1.04 \times 1.04 \times 1.04 \times 1.04 \times 1.04 = \$7{,}299.92$$

Note that because we are working with money, we round to the nearest cent. Finish the calculation by plugging that into the formula:

$$\text{compound interest} = \$7{,}299.92 - \$6{,}000$$
$$= \$1{,}299.92$$

You could also use the simple interest formula to find the compound interest. It is a little more time-consuming, but it is an easier formula with which to work.

To use the simple interest formula to calculate compound interest, you apply the formula for each period and add the interest from the previous period to the principal amount for the next period. Sounds confusing, right? It really isn't! Let's look at how the simple interest formula works for calculating compound interest, using the same loan that we used for compound interest.

For the first year, plug the numbers into the simple interest formula:

$$\text{first-year interest} = \$6{,}000 \times 4\% \times 1 \text{ year}$$
$$= \$240$$

Add the interest to the principal so that the second-year interest will be calculated on the original principal plus the first year's interest:

$$\text{second-year interest} = (\$6{,}000 + \$240) \times 4\% \times 1$$
$$= \$6{,}240 \times 4\% \times 1$$
$$= \$249.60$$

Continue this process for the remaining years:

$$\text{third-year interest} = (\$6{,}240 + \$249.60) \times 4\% \times 1$$
$$= \$6{,}489.60 \times 4\% \times 1$$
$$= \$259.58$$

$$\text{fourth-year interest} = (\$6{,}489.60 + \$259.58) \times 4\% \times 1$$
$$= \$6{,}749.18 \times 4\% \times 1$$
$$= \$269.97$$

$$\text{fifth-year interest} = (\$6{,}749.18 + \$269.97) \times 4\% \times 1$$
$$= \$7{,}019.15 \times 4\% \times 1$$
$$= \$280.77$$

The last step is to add all of the interest amounts to find the final total of the compounded interest:

$$\$240 + \$249.60 + \$259.58 + \$269.97 + \$280.77 = \$1{,}299.92$$

You get the same answer using the simple interest formula to calculate compound interest as you did using the compound interest formula. The formula that you use is a matter of preference.

COMPARING SIMPLE AND COMPOUND INTEREST

Let's look at an example of how the two types of interest, using the same rate and same length of time, would affect a deposit: a $20,000 deposit for two years at 4% interest.

Simple Interest

Remember our formula from before:

$$\text{simple interest} = \text{principal} \times \text{rate} \times \text{time}$$

The first step is to plug the numbers in, remembering to use a decimal number for the interest rate.

$$\text{simple interest} = \$20{,}000 \times 0.04 \times 2$$

Now, perform the multiplication to get your answer.

$$\text{simple interest} = \$1{,}600$$

At the end of the period, your $20,000 deposit would have grown to $21,600. How much would it grow to if the interest were compounded annually?

Compound Interest

In this example, we'll use the formula for compound interest, even though you could figure out this problem using the simple interest formula, as explained earlier. Here is the compound interest formula:

$$\text{compound interest} = \left[\text{principal} \times \left(1 + \frac{\text{rate}}{n}\right)^{\text{periods} \times n}\right] - \text{principal}$$

(In the formula, n equals the number of times that the interest is compounded per year.)

Our equation for this example would look like this:

$$\begin{aligned}\text{compound interest} &= [\$20{,}000 \times (1 + 0.04)^2] - \$20{,}000\\ &= (\$20{,}000 \times 1.04^2) - \$20{,}000\\ &= (\$20{,}000 \times 1.0816) - \$20{,}000\\ &= \$21{,}632 - \$20{,}000\\ &= \$1{,}632\end{aligned}$$

When compounded annually, the interest on this deposit would be $1,632, making the total amount you would have at the end of the period $21,632. Compare this with what the deposit earned using simple interest. You can see that the deposit earned $32 more using compound interest than using simple interest.

HOW MUCH TO DEPOSIT?

Now that we've covered the basics of compound and simple interest, let's shake it up a bit. Let's look at how you would calculate how much you would need to deposit if you know how much you'd like to have at the end of the period and you know the interest rate. We'll assume that you would like to have $30,000 in five years. The best interest rate available is 6%, compounded annually. To calculate the amount you'd need to deposit, you just need to rethink the formula.

The compound interest formula is:

$$\text{compound interest} = \left[\text{principal} \times \left(1 + \frac{\text{rate}}{n}\right)^{\text{periods} \times n}\right] - \text{principal}$$

To figure out what principal you would need—how much you would need to deposit—you would set up the formula like this:

$$\text{principal} = \text{future value} \div \left(1 + \frac{\text{rate}}{n}\right)^{\text{periods} \times n}$$

You can see that what we did here was to reverse the formula. We pulled out the principal from the original formula and now we're performing division using the future value of the loan. Let's plug in the numbers to finish this problem:

$$\begin{aligned} \text{principal} &= \$30{,}000 \div (1 + 0.06)^5 \\ &= \$30{,}000 \div (1.06)^5 \\ &= \$30{,}000 \div 1.3382 \\ &= \$22{,}418.17 \end{aligned}$$

Based on this calculation, to end up with $30,000 after five years, you would need to deposit $22,418.17, which you can easily round down to $22,418.

How much would you need to deposit if everything was the same, except the interest was compounded quarterly? Start out by plugging the numbers into your formula, remembering to change the compounding periods.

$$\text{principal} = \$30{,}000 \div \left(1 + \frac{0.06}{4}\right)^{20}$$

The compounding periods amount was increased to 20 from 5 because the interest is compounded quarterly, or four times a year. Now, finish the problem:

$$\begin{aligned} \text{principal} &= \$30{,}000 \div (1 + 0.015)^{20} \\ &= \$30{,}000 \div 1.015^{20} \\ &= \$30{,}000 \div 1.3468 \\ &= \$22{,}275.02 \end{aligned}$$

With interest that compounds quarterly, you'd need to deposit $22,275.02 (or $22,275 when you round down) to end up with $30,000. That is $143 less than what you would need with only annual compounding!

PRACTICE QUIZ

1. An entrepreneur has applied for a $40,000 loan for her start-up business. Which set of terms would be the most cost-efficient for her?
a. a three-year loan at 7%, compounded quarterly
b. a three-year loan at 6%, compounded monthly
c. a four-year loan at 6%, compounded annually

2. A company borrows $10,000 for one year with a compounding interest rate of 5% per month. How much does the company pay back at the end of the loan period?

How much would you need to deposit to end up with $40,000 if the terms were as follows?

3. 4% interest, compounded monthly, for three years
4. 6% interest, compounded quarterly, for five years
5. 5% interest, compounded annually, for five years

Calculate the simple interest for the following:

6. a $2,700 deposit for two years at 4.5% interest
7. a loan of $55,000 for six months at 8% interest
8. a loan of $15,000 for three months at 7.5% interest

Calculate the compound interest for the following:

9. a $42,000 loan for five years at 9% interest, compounded quarterly
10. a $22,000 deposit for two years at 4% interest, compounded monthly
11. a $9,000 loan for one year at 6% interest, compounded monthly

CHAPTER SIX

Depreciation

Almost every business asset—anything that a business owns, such as equipment, vehicles, office furniture, and the like—loses value over time because of wear and tear, because of age, or because it becomes outdated. In other words, the assets depreciate. Let's say your company bought new computers for all employees in 2007. As soon as the computers went into service, they became assets for the company, but they also lost some value. Every year the company owns them, the computers lose more value until they finally have no value to the company at all. This reduction in value must be measured, and the measurement is called depreciation.

Depreciation is a noncash expense involving the periodic, systematic reduction in value of an asset over the course of its useful life. However, it does not indicate a decline in the *market* value of an asset.

Depreciation can be calculated in several ways, which this chapter will demonstrate. You will learn the causes of depreciation, along with the formulas for straight-line depreciation, the units of production method, the sum of the years' digits method, the declining balance method, and the double declining balance method.

CAUSES OF DEPRECIATION

The two primary ways in which assets can depreciate are called functional depreciation and physical depreciation. Functional depreciation means that the asset cannot perform the required function due to becoming outmoded or having inadequate design. This can occur when technological advances make the asset obsolete or a company's increased demands for productivity exceed the asset's capacity. For example, a printer may be able to print 20 pages per minute, a capacity

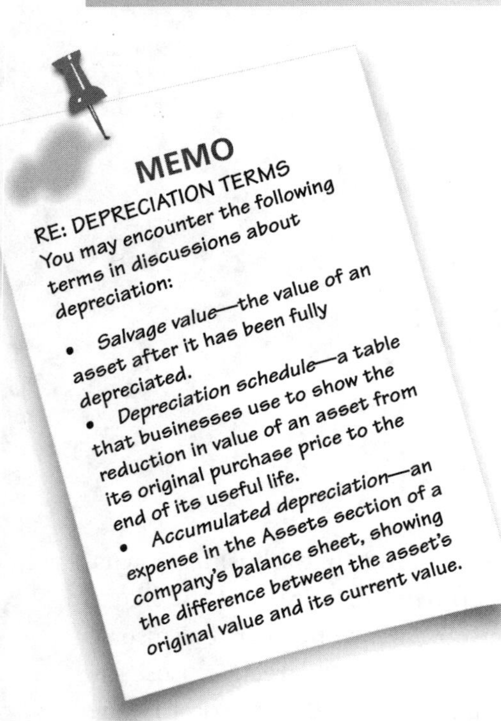

that is fine for a particular company for the first year. In the second year, however, new clients require the company to increase its output. Now, the company needs a printer that can print 50 pages per minute. The original printer, the asset, has now lost its value to the company because it can't perform the required function.

Physical depreciation refers to the wear and tear on an asset. An asset may become more costly to operate because it requires repairs. Or the wear and tear may cause slower output. Over time, almost all assets will lose value because of physical depreciation.

CALCULATING DEPRECIATION

In order to find the depreciation for assets, you need to know three things:

1. the initial cost
2. the useful life
3. the expected salvage value at the end of the useful life

The Internal Revenue Service (IRS) and state revenue authorities all have rules regarding depreciation and the methods for calculating depreciation for different assets. Check the publications from these organizations before calculating the depreciation of any assets. Additionally, trade publications and insurance data can be helpful when estimating the useful life and salvage value of assets.

If an asset will have little or no salvage value, the entire initial cost can be spread out over its useful life using depreciation. If an asset is expected to have some salvage value, then the difference between the initial value and the salvage value can be spread out over its useful life using depreciation.

Once you have the necessary information for finding the depreciation for your assets, you can use one of the five primary depreciation methods.

Straight-Line Depreciation

Straight-line depreciation is the simplest and most common form of depreciation. With straight-line depreciation, the annual depreciation value is the same each year for each year of the asset's useful life. The formula for straight-line depreciation is:

$$\text{depreciation amount} = (P - V) \div Y$$

where P = initial price
V = salvage value
Y = years of useful life

Suppose your company has a fax machine that was purchased for $550. It is expected to have a useful life of three years, and the expected salvage value is $75. Here's how you would calculate the annual depreciation value using the straight-line method:

$$\begin{aligned}\text{depreciation amount} &= (\$550 - \$75) \div 3 \\ &= \$475 \div 3 \\ &= \$158.33 \text{ (when rounded to the nearest cent)}\end{aligned}$$

For each year of the useful life of the fax machine, the depreciation amount would be $158.33.

Units of Production Method

This depreciation method is based on the asset's lifetime capacity to do work. The units can be measured in whatever way is appropriate for the asset: hours of operation, miles, number of items produced, and so on. With this method, the annual depreciation value changes based on the amount that the asset is used. It is the most accurate method for matching depreciation with actual usage. The formula for the units of production method of depreciation is:

$$\text{depreciation amount} = (P - V) \times (U \div L)$$

where P = initial price
V = salvage value
U = units used in the current period (for example, a fiscal year)
L = expected lifetime units capacity of the asset

Let's look at an example of how you would use the units of production method. A company purchases a generator for $12,000 and expects that it will be used on and off. There are no set hours that the generator will be used each year, but the company does expect that the generator has a useful life of 25,000 hours, after which it will have a salvage value of $1,000. This would be a good asset to depreciate using the units of production method, because some years the usage could be very high and some years it could be low. This is what the depreciation might look like for the first three years, assuming the generator was used for 275 hours the first year, 4,075 hours the second year, and 1,242 hours the third year:

$$\begin{aligned}\text{depreciation amount (year one)} &= (\$12{,}000 - \$1{,}000) \times (275 \div 25{,}000)\\ &= \$11{,}000 \times 0.011\\ &= \$121\end{aligned}$$

The amount that would be depreciated in the first year would be $121.

$$\begin{aligned}\text{depreciation amount (year two)} &= (\$12{,}000 - \$1{,}000) \times (4{,}075 \div 25{,}000)\\ &= \$11{,}000 \times 0.163\\ &= \$1{,}793\end{aligned}$$

Because the usage was much higher in the second year, the depreciation was, too. For the second year, the depreciation would be $1,793.

$$\begin{aligned}\text{depreciation amount (year three)} &= (\$12{,}000 - \$1{,}000) \times (1{,}242 \div 25{,}000)\\ &= \$11{,}000 \times 0.049\\ &= \$539\end{aligned}$$

The usage went down in the third year and the depreciation followed. You can see from this example that this method matches depreciation to usage more accurately than other methods do. However, it is useful only when you know how many units you expect an asset to produce in all and how many it produces during a set period.

Sum of the Years' Digits Method

The sum of the years' digits method of depreciation is an accelerated depreciation method. This method assumes that an asset loses most of its value in the first few years of use. With this method, the annual depreciation value decreases each year. The formula for the sum of the years' digits method of depreciation is:

$$\text{depreciation amount (for the given year)} = (P - V) \times [(Y + 1 - C) \div S]$$

where P = initial price
V = salvage value
Y = years of useful life
C = current year
S = sum of years of useful life

To calculate the sum of the years of useful life, determine the number of years you will use an asset. Then, count back to 1 from that number and add the digits together. It sounds more complicated than it is. Let's say you need to depreciate a vehicle that you expect to have in service for seven years. Add the digits together by counting back from 7 to 1 to get: $7 + 6 + 5 + 4 + 3 + 2 + 1 = 28$.

The S in the formula would be 28.

To finish this example, let's say the vehicle cost $20,000 and the expected salvage value is $5,000. We can plug the numbers into the formula to calculate the value for the first year:

$$\begin{aligned}\text{depreciation amount (year one)} &= (\$20{,}000 - \$5{,}000) \times [(7 + 1 - 1) \div 28] \\ &= \$15{,}000 \times (7 \div 28) \\ &= \$3{,}750\end{aligned}$$

The second year would look like this:

$$\begin{aligned}\text{depreciation amount (year two)} &= (\$20{,}000 - \$5{,}000) \times [(7 + 1 - 2) \div 28] \\ &= \$15{,}000 \times (6 \div 28) \\ &= \$3{,}214.29\end{aligned}$$

The remaining years:

$$\begin{aligned}\text{depreciation amount (year three)} &= (\$20{,}000 - \$5{,}000) \times [(7 + 1 - 3) \div 28] \\ &= \$15{,}000 \times (5 \div 28) \\ &= \$2{,}678.57\end{aligned}$$

$$\begin{aligned}\text{depreciation amount (year four)} &= (\$20{,}000 - \$5{,}000) \times [(7 + 1 - 4) \div 28] \\ &= \$15{,}000 \times (4 \div 28) \\ &= \$2{,}142.86\end{aligned}$$

$$\begin{aligned}\text{depreciation amount (year five)} &= (\$20{,}000 - \$5{,}000) \times [(7 + 1 - 5) \div 28] \\ &= \$15{,}000 \times (3 \div 28) \\ &= \$1{,}607.14\end{aligned}$$

$$\begin{aligned}\text{depreciation amount (year six)} &= (\$20{,}000 - \$5{,}000) \times [(7 + 1 - 6) \div 28] \\ &= \$15{,}000 \times (2 \div 28) \\ &= \$1{,}071.43\end{aligned}$$

$$\begin{aligned}\text{depreciation amount (year seven)} &= (\$20{,}000 - \$5{,}000) \times [(7 + 1 - 7) \div 28] \\ &= \$15{,}000 \times (1 \div 28) \\ &= \$535.71\end{aligned}$$

Declining Balance Method

The declining balance method is another accelerated depreciation method. As with the sum of the years' digits, this method assumes that an asset loses most of its value in the first few years of use and the annual depreciation value decreases each year. The declining balance method depreciates an asset at one and a half times the rate of straight-line depreciation. The formula for this method is:

$$\text{depreciation amount} = B \times (1.5 \div Y)$$

where B = current book value
Y = years of useful life

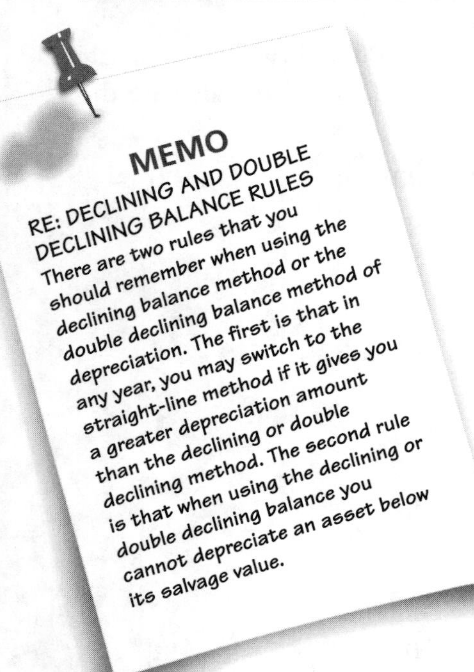

With the declining balance method, you must know the current book value of your asset. Let's say a company has a delivery van that was purchased for $32,000. It has been in service for two of the eight years of its useful life, and its current book value is $26,000. The salvage value is $3,000. We'll plug the numbers into the formula to calculate the depreciation amount for year two:

$$\begin{aligned} &\text{depreciation amount (year two)} \\ &= \$26{,}000 \times (1.5 \div 8) \\ &= \$26{,}000 \times 0.1875 \\ &= \$4{,}875 \end{aligned}$$

The depreciation amount for year two, using the declining balance method, would be $4,875. But, we're not done! You want to use the declining balance method of depreciation only when it gives you a greater depreciation amount than the straight-line method. So, we need to calculate the depreciation using the straight-line method and compare the results to determine which method would be appropriate to use.

Here is the formula for straight-line depreciation:

$$\text{depreciation amount} = (P - V) \div Y$$

where P = initial price
V = salvage value
Y = years of useful life

Using the same figures, the straight-line depreciation for year two would look like this:

$$\begin{aligned} \text{depreciation amount (year two)} &= (\$32{,}000 - \$3{,}000) \div 8 \\ &= \$29{,}000 \div 8 \\ &= \$3{,}625 \end{aligned}$$

Now we have the two depreciation amounts for year two. Using the declining balance method, the amount would be $4,875. Using the straight-line method, where an asset depreciates by the same value each year, the amount would be $3,625. So, in this case, you would use the declining balance method because the depreciation amount is greater than it would be using the straight-line method.

Double Declining Balance Method

This is another accelerated depreciation method. The double declining balance method depreciates at twice the rate of straight-line depreciation. The formula for this method is:

$$\text{depreciation amount} = B \times (2 \div Y)$$

where B = current book value
Y = years of useful life

Let's take a look at the declining balance example, but use the double declining balance method of depreciation.

$$\begin{aligned}\text{depreciation amount (year two)} &= \$26{,}000 \times (2 \div 8)\\ &= \$26{,}000 \times 0.25\\ &= \$6{,}500\end{aligned}$$

The depreciation amount using the double declining balance method would be $6,500. As with the declining balance method, you need to compare your result with that of the straight-line method. Because we have already calculated the depreciation amount using that method, we know that the depreciation amount would be $3,625. This is less than the depreciation amount would be using the double declining balance method, so you would go with the $6,500 depreciation amount calculated using double declining balance.

PRACTICE QUIZ

Calculate the annual depreciation amount for the following items using the straight-line method:

1. a vehicle purchased for $37,500 that has a useful life of six years and a salvage value of $4,000
2. a photocopier with a useful life of three years, purchased for $880, with a salvage value of $100
3. three computers purchased for $2,045 each, with useful lives of two years and a total salvage value of $425

Calculate the annual depreciation amount for the following items using the units of production method:

4. a binding machine purchased for $83,000 with a salvage value of $12,000, lifetime unit production capacity of 750,000 bindings, and production of 18,550 bindings in the current year
5. a scanner with a lifetime capacity of 50,000 scans, purchased for $11,720, and having a salvage value of $3,450. It produced 1,060 scans in the current year.

6. a fleet of six identical cars, each purchased for $25,200 and each with a useful life of 75,000 miles and salvage value of $6,300. In the current accounting year, car A had 12,305 miles, car B had 10,170 miles, car C had 14,201 miles, car D had 14,220 miles, car E had 12,992 miles, and car F had 11,550 miles.

Calculate the annual depreciation amount for the following items using the sum of the years' digits method:

7. a generator with a purchase price of $7,399, a salvage value of $600, and a useful life of nine years. The generator is in its fourth year of service.
8. that same generator in its seventh year of service
9. a vehicle in its second year of service with a useful life of five years and a salvage value of $3,800, purchased for $13,700
10. that same vehicle in its fifth year of service

Calculate the annual depreciation amount for the following items using the declining balance method:

11. a truck purchased for $41,500 with a salvage value of $9,000 and a current book value of $37,000. The expected useful life of the truck is seven years, and it is in its first year of service.
12. a recording system purchased for $43,650 with a current book value of $21,500 and a salvage value of $9,000. It is in its sixth year of service and has a useful life of 15 years.

Calculate the annual depreciation amount for the following items using the double declining balance method:

13. ten laptop computers purchased for $1,735 each. They each have a current book value of $800 and a salvage value of $200. They are in their second year of service with a useful life of four years.
14. a projector in its third year of service with a current book value of $2,200. It was purchased for $5,800 and has a salvage value of $900 and a useful life of 12 years.

CHAPTER SEVEN

Markup and Markdown

Setting the right price for a product or service is a key step toward making a profit. If a business sets the price of an item too low, it risks not covering all expenses or not making enough profit. On the other hand, if it sets the price of an item too high, it risks not being able to move enough units or sign enough contracts for service to be profitable. As the saying goes, the best price for a product really is the price the consumer is willing to pay!

This chapter covers the basics of markup and markdown, demonstrating how they are calculated and providing an introduction to some pricing models.

MARKUP

Markup is a simple concept. It occurs when a business charges an amount for a product or service that is greater than the cost to the business to produce that product or service. The concept may be simple, but determining the right amount of markup can be tricky. The two primary forms of markup are markup from cost and markup from price.

Before we move on to explaining the forms of markup, let's be clear about two terms: *price* and *cost*. The price of a product or service is the amount that a company charges after it applies a markup. The cost of a product or service is what it actually costs a company to produce the product or perform the service.

Markup from Cost

Markup from cost can also be referred to as cost plus markup. With markup from cost, the markup rate is expressed as a percentage. In order to determine your price, you need to know the cost of your product or service, and you need to know what your markup rate is. If, for example, you wish to make 20% on all products that you sell, this would be your markup rate. Here is how you would calculate the price of a product that costs $7.50 with a 20% markup:

$$\begin{aligned} \text{price} &= \text{cost} \times (1 + \text{markup rate}) \\ &= \$7.50 \times (1 + 0.20) \\ &= \$7.50 \times 1.20 \\ &= \$9.00 \end{aligned}$$

Notice that we express the markup rate of 20% as a decimal. To realize a 20% markup on a product that costs $7.50, your price would be $9.00.

Let's look at another example. Suppose the cost of a service is $55 and your markup rate is 30%. What price would you have to charge for your service?

$$\begin{aligned} \text{price} &= \text{cost} \times (1 + \text{markup rate}) \\ &= \$55 \times (1 + 0.30) \\ &= \$55 \times 1.30 \\ &= \$71.50 \end{aligned}$$

You would need to charge $71.50 for your service if your markup rate is 30%.

Let's look at things a different way. You can calculate your markup rate if you know your cost and your price, just by rearranging the formula:

$$\text{markup rate} = (\text{price} \div \text{cost}) - 1$$

For example, if your company charges $110 per hour for on-site service calls and you know that your cost for each hour is $82, what is your markup rate?

Plug the known amounts into the formula from above:

$$\begin{aligned} \text{markup rate} &= (\$110 \div \$82) - 1 \\ &= 1.341 - 1 \\ &= 0.341\text{, or } 34\% \text{ (rounded)} \end{aligned}$$

You would round off the result and express it as a percentage, because markup rates are always expressed as percentages. So, if your cost per hour is $82 and you charge $110, your markup rate is approximately 34%.

Similarly, you can calculate your cost if you know your markup rate and your price:

$$\text{cost} = \text{price} \div (1 + \text{markup rate})$$

Here's an example. Suppose you want to know if your costs are generally higher or lower than those of your main competitor, which you've learned uses a 30% markup rate on all products that it sells. If the price of one of this competitor's products is $27.99, what is the cost?

Use the formula for finding cost from before and plug in the numbers that you know:

$$\text{cost} = \$27.99 \div (1 + 0.30)$$

Notice again that we express the markup rate of 30% as a decimal. Now, complete the equation.

$$\begin{aligned}\text{cost} &= \$27.99 \div 1.30 \\ &= \$21.53 \text{ (when rounded to the nearest cent)}\end{aligned}$$

Your competitor's cost is $21.53. Now you can compare your costs to that to see if they are higher or lower.

Here's another example. A store is buying products from a distributor that have a suggested list price of $39.99. The store wants to sell the products for that price, and it requires that all products sold have at least a 25% markup. What would be the most that the store would pay to the distributor?

To figure this out, use the same formula we just used:

$$\text{cost} = \text{price} \div (1 + \text{markup rate})$$

You know the price that the store wishes to charge and you know its markup rate, so put those into the formula:

$$\begin{aligned}\text{cost} &= \$39.99 \div (1 + 0.25) \\ &= \$39.99 \div 1.25 \\ &= \$31.99\end{aligned}$$

In order for the store to sell the product at $39.99 and make a 25% markup, the store must purchase the item from the distributor for $31.99.

Markup from Price

A different way of looking at markup is markup from price. With markup from price, the markup rate is a percentage of the selling price, rather than a percentage that is added onto the cost.

To calculate the selling price of an item using markup from price, you would use this formula:

$$\text{price} = \text{cost} \div (1 - \text{markup rate})$$

We'll look at an example. If a company has an item with a cost of $14 and a markup rate of 25%, here's how you would calculate the price:

$$\begin{aligned}\text{price} &= \$14 \div (1 - 0.25) \\ &= \$14 \div 0.75 \\ &= \$18.67 \text{ (when rounded to the nearest cent)}\end{aligned}$$

The selling price of the item would be $18.67.

As with markup from cost, you can calculate the markup rate or the cost, provided you know the other two amounts. So, to calculate cost using the markup from price method you would use this formula:

$$\text{cost} = \text{price} \times (1 - \text{markup rate})$$

Suppose your company charges $50 for its product and you use a 25% markup based on that selling price. What is your cost? To figure it out, plug the known amounts into the formula.

$$\begin{aligned}\text{cost} &= \$50 \times (1 - 0.25)\\ &= \$50 \times 0.75\\ &= \$37.50\end{aligned}$$

Your cost for the product that is priced at $50 is $37.50. Now, what if you know the cost and selling price but not the markup rate? There is a formula for that, of course!

$$\text{markup rate} = 1 - (\text{cost} \div \text{price})$$

Here is an example of how to calculate the markup rate for markup from price. If a consulting company charges $35.95 per hour for a consultant whose cost is $22 per hour, you would calculate the markup rate like this:

$$\begin{aligned}\text{markup rate} &= 1 - (\$22 \div \$35.95)\\ &= 1 - 0.61\\ &= 0.39\text{, or } 39\%\end{aligned}$$

The markup rate would be 39%.

One advantage for companies that use markup from price is that they can claim that a smaller percentage of the price is markup than if they used markup from cost. Let's look at why this is the case:

Say that Company A uses markup from cost to price its products and Company B uses markup from price. Each company sells an item that costs $12 and is priced at $15.99. Here is how the markup rate differs using the two methods:

Company A: Markup from Cost

$$\begin{aligned}\text{markup rate} &= (\text{price} \div \text{cost}) - 1\\ &= (\$15.99 \div \$12) - 1\\ &= 1.3325 - 1\\ &= 0.3325\text{, or } 33\% \text{ (rounded)}\end{aligned}$$

Company A's markup rate is approximately 33%. Now let's look at Company B.

Company B: Markup from Price

$$\begin{aligned}\text{markup rate} &= 1 - (\text{cost} \div \text{price})\\ &= 1 - (\$12 \div \$15.99)\\ &= 1 - 0.75\\ &= 0.25\text{, or } 25\%\end{aligned}$$

Company B's markup rate is 25%.

Although both companies have the same cost and charge the same price, Company A's markup rate based on cost is higher than Company B's rate based on markup from price.

MEMO

RE: RETAIL PRICING STRATEGIES

Some common retail pricing strategies include:

- competitive pricing below competition—a price that beats the competitor's price; a strategy that works when a company can buy at the best prices
- competitive pricing above competition—a price that is higher than the competitor's price; a strategy that works when location, exclusivity, or special service warrants the higher price
- psychological pricing—a price that is based on popular price points and what consumers perceive to be the value of the product; may also be referred to as "value-based pricing"
- multiple pricing—a price that involves selling a number of units for one price, such as three for $20; a strategy that works well when a company's priority is moving a large number of units
- going rate—a price that is the same as your competitor's price

MARKDOWNS

Now that we've covered markup, we'll move on to markdown. Markdown is the reduction in price of a product or service based on a percentage of the original price. Markdown is not computed on cost. The resulting price of a markdown is called—surprise!—the sale price. Generally speaking, companies mark down their prices to increase sales during a specific period or to clear out inventory.

As with markup, markdown is expressed as a percentage, and you can calculate the sale (markdown) price, original price, or markdown rate provided you know the other two amounts. We'll start with how to calculate the sale price. The formula is:

$$\text{sale price} = \text{original price} \times (1 - \text{markdown rate})$$

For example, if a company is offering a year-end special on laptops that were originally priced at $1,299 but have now been marked down 30%, what would the sale price be?

$$\begin{aligned}\text{sale price} &= \$1{,}299 \times (1 - 0.30)\\ &= \$1{,}299 \times 0.70\\ &= \$909.30\end{aligned}$$

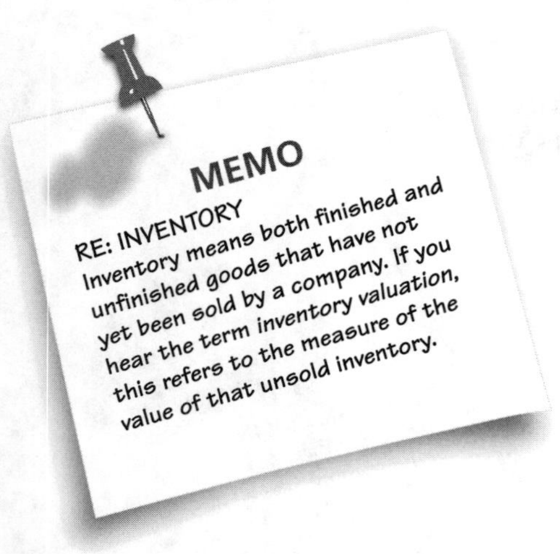

Here's another example. Suppose a wholesaler is offering a 40% markdown to retailers who purchase at least 500 units of a product. For retailers who purchase between 300 and 499 units, the wholesaler is offering a 30% markdown. Your company had planned to purchase 400 units but is now considering increasing its order because of the higher markdown. If the original price of the product is $71, what will your company's costs be for 400 units and for 500 units?

To determine the total cost in each case, you need to calculate the sale price for each scenario and then multiply that by the number of units in your order. First, let's start with the 30% markdown:

$$\begin{aligned}\text{sale price} &= \text{original price} \times (1 - \text{markdown rate}) \\ &= \$71 \times (1 - 0.30) \\ &= \$71 \times 0.70 \\ &= \$49.70\end{aligned}$$

The sale price at a 30% markdown rate would be $49.70. Because your company would purchase 400 units at this price, the total cost would be 400 × $49.70, or $19,880.

Now, let's change the markdown rate to 40%:

$$\begin{aligned}\text{sale price} &= \text{original price} \times (1 - \text{markdown rate}) \\ &= \$71 \times (1 - 0.40) \\ &= \$71 \times 0.60 \\ &= \$42.60\end{aligned}$$

In order to receive the 40% markdown rate, your company would need to purchase 500 units. So, the total cost at that rate would be 500 × $42.60, or $21,300, only $1,420 more than your company would pay for 400 units.

Now that you have the total cost for each scenario, you would be able to determine whether it makes good business sense to purchase 400 or 500 units.

You can calculate the original price if you know the sale price and the markdown rate. Here is the formula that you would use:

$$\text{original price} = \text{sale price} \div (1 - \text{markdown rate})$$

If the sale price for an item is \$16.96 and the advertised markdown rate is 15%, what was the original price?

original price = \$16.96 ÷ (1 – 0.15)
= \$16.96 ÷ 0.85
= \$19.95 (when rounded to the nearest cent)

The original price of the item was \$19.95.

Let's look at how to find the markdown rate. In order to find the markdown rate, you need to know the sale price and the original price. The formula is:

markdown rate = 1 – (sale price ÷ original price)

Here's an example. If a company originally sold a product for \$59.99 and planned to offer it at a sale price of \$39.99, what markdown rate could it promote in its weekly sales flyer?

To answer this, plug the known amounts into the formula for finding the markdown rate.

markdown rate = 1 – (\$39.99 ÷ \$59.99)
= 1 – 0.67 (rounded)
= 0.33 (rounded)

Convert the decimal number in your answer to a percent to get the markdown rate: 0.33 = 33%. So, the company could advertise that it was offering 33% off its original price.

Let's look at another example using an original price of \$450 and a sale price of \$299.

markdown rate = 1 – (\$299 ÷ \$450)
= 1 – 0.66 (rounded)
= 0.34 (rounded)

The markdown rate when a product is reduced from \$450 to \$299 is 34%.

BREAKEVEN POINT

There is one issue that you need to consider when working with markups and markdowns in setting prices: the breakeven point.

The breakeven point is where costs and income (or gains and losses, sales and revenue) are equal. At this point, there is no profit but there is no loss, either. Basically, the breakeven point is the lowest amount of sales that a company needs to achieve to stay afloat. After reaching the breakeven point, anything sold beyond it will generate profit for the company.

The amount that a product or service is marked up (or marked down) will have an effect on the breakeven point. So, you should look at your breakeven point in tandem with price setting.

You can use this formula to reveal your breakeven point:

breakeven point = total fixed costs ÷ (selling price – variable costs)

In this formula, the selling price is per unit, as are the variable costs.

We'll work through an example to show how to find the breakeven point. A start-up company that sells children's T-shirts has set the price for the shirts at $10 each. The total fixed costs are $4,722 and the variable costs per unit are approximately $2.50. So, how many T-shirts does the company need to sell to break even?

breakeven point = $4,722 ÷ ($10 – $2.50)
= $4,722 ÷ $7.50
= 629.6 units

In this example, the company needs to sell 630 T-shirts to break even.

Let's say a company expects that it will be able to sell 30,000 units of its product in one year. The total fixed costs are $730,000 and the variable costs per unit are $28. The company has looked at competitors' prices and decided to set its price at $70 per unit. Will it be able to do this and break even?

First, we need to calculate the breakeven point and then compare that to the company's sales projection.

breakeven point = $730,000 ÷ ($70 – $28)
= $730,000 ÷ $42
= 17,380.95238
= 17,381 units (when rounded to the nearest whole unit)

Now, compare the sales projection to the breakeven point. The company projects that it will sell 30,000 units. That is greater than the breakeven point of 17,381 units, so, yes, it can set the price at $70 per unit and break even. In this case, the company will make a profit!

PRACTICE QUIZ

Use markup from cost for questions 1 to 8:

1. What is the markup rate on a computer that costs $722 and has a selling price of $1,199?
2. If the markup on a pen that costs $2.25 is $0.75, what is the markup rate?

3. What is the cost of a blouse that sells for $64 and has a markup rate of 76%?
4. What is the cost of a product that sells for $55.44 and has a markup rate of 27.2%?
5. What is the price per hour for a service that has a cost of $58.79 per hour and a markup rate of 80.9%?
6. What is the selling price of an item with a cost of $50.51 and a markup rate of 6.7%?
7. If the price of a bracelet is $89.10 and the cost is $28.44, what is the markup rate?
8. What price would you set for an item if your cost was $34.54 and you were using a markup rate of 52.5%?

Use markup from price for questions 9 to 17:

9. What is the price of an item where the cost is $41.40 and the markup rate is 34%?
10. What is the markup rate for an item with a cost of $24.99 and a price of $36.75?
11. If a company's markup rate is 31.7%, what would be the price of an item that has a cost of $10.87?
12. What is the cost for an item that sells for $60.08 and has a markup rate of 32.2%?
13. What is the price of a handbag with a cost of $66.65 and a markup rate of 76.9%?
14. What is the markup rate for a fixed-price dinner with a cost of $49.50 and a menu price of $90?
15. What is a company's cost for an item that sells for $15.96 and has a markup rate of 24.5%?
16. What is the cost of an item that sells for $100 and has a markup rate of 40%?
17. What is the markup rate for an item with a cost of $8.45 and a price of $30.70?

Use markdown for questions 18 to 23:

18. A sofa that had originally been priced at $900 was marked down by 20% and then by 30%. What was the final selling price?
19. If a wholesaler originally charged $60.35 per unit for an item and marked it down by 35.8%, what sale price would it offer retailers?
20. If the sale price of a pair of jeans is $72.89 and the advertised markdown is 55%, what was the original price?
21. What is the markdown rate if the original price of an item was $137.54 and the sale price is $64.65?
22. What is the sale price for a plate that originally was priced at $29.99 and has been marked down 73.5%?

23. Find the markdown rate of an item that has a sale price of $27.17 and an original price of $89.

Use breakeven point for questions 24 and 25:

24. A company has set the price for an item at $30. The total fixed costs are $15,000 and the variable costs per unit are $17. What is the breakeven point?
25. Will a company break even if it sells 10,000 units of a $15 product that has total fixed costs of $27,000 and variable costs per unit of $11?

CHAPTER **EIGHT**

Introduction to Financial Statements

There are four basic types of financial statements: the balance sheet, the income statement or profit and loss (P&L) statement, the statement of retained earnings, and the statement of cash flow. These statements document the financial activities of a business. They show the state of a business's financial affairs and, one hopes, how profitable a business is.

This chapter will give you an introduction to financial statements so you can understand what each one covers. In the next chapter, we'll go into more detail on the most popular financial statement, the P&L or income statement.

THE BALANCE SHEET

Think of a balance sheet as a snapshot that provides an overview of a company's financial condition *at a single point in time*. It differs from the other types of financial statements, which report on financial activities *over a period of time*. A balance sheet covers a company's assets, liabilities, and the owners' or shareholders' equity, and is called a balance sheet because the assets must equal the liabilities plus equity, *or be balanced*.

A balance sheet consists of two parts: The first part shows the company's assets, and the other shows its liabilities plus equity. When reading a balance sheet, it is important to understand these parts.

Assets

There are two types of assets: current and fixed (or noncurrent).

Current assets are those that can be easily converted into cash. They include actual cash (such as checks and nonrestricted bank accounts) and cash equivalents (such as Treasury bills or money market accounts), accounts receivable, and inventory. Fixed, or noncurrent, assets are those that cannot be easily converted into cash. They include tangible assets like computers, vehicles, or real estate and intangible assets such as human capital, goodwill, and patents.

The phrase *total fixed assets* means the total value of all the fixed assets of a company, minus any accumulated depreciation. The phrase *total assets* means the total amount of the current and the fixed assets of a company.

Liabilities

Liabilities are the financial obligations of a company. There are two types: current liabilities and long-term liabilities.

Current liabilities are those financial obligations that must be paid within one year. These might include mortgage payments, accrued wages for employees that have not yet been paid, and other loan payments or bills that are due within the year. In contrast, long-term liabilities are those financial obligations that are due one year or more from the date of the balance sheet.

Also included in liabilities is the owners' (or shareholders') equity. Owners' equity is the initial investment that the owners made in the company plus any retained earnings, such as dividend payments, that have been reinvested in the company. The owners' equity is combined with the liabilities on the balance sheet to become the total liabilities and owners' equity. This amount should be equal to, or balance, the total assets.

The format for a balance sheet is:

total assets = total liabilities + owners' (or shareholders') equity

In greater detail, the format looks like this:

current assets
+ total fixed (or noncurrent) assets (minus accumulated depreciation)
total assets

current liabilities
+ long-term liabilities
+ owners' equity
total liabilities and owners' equity

total assets = total liabilities and owners' equity

Let's look at a sample balance sheet to gain a better understanding of this financial statement.

TOPSY TOYS
Balance Sheet
For the Month Ending January 31, 2008

Assets		*Liabilities and Owners' Equity*	
Current Assets		**Liabilities**	
Cash	$ 30,000	Current Liabilities	$ 70,000
Accounts Receivable	85,000	Long-Term Liabilities	160,000
Other	8,000		
Inventory	65,000	**Total Liabilities**	230,000
Property and Equipment			
Building	205,000	**Owners' Equity**	
Furniture	55,000	Paid-In Capital	200,000
Equipment	85,000	Retained Earnings	120,000
Intangibles			
Goodwill	15,000	**Total Owners' Equity**	320,000
Other Assets	2,000		
Total Assets	**$550,000**	**Total Liabilities and Owners' Equity**	**$550,000**

As you can see, the total assets and total liabilities and owner's equity lines are equal. Thus, we have a properly balanced balance sheet!

MEMO
RE: INCOME VERSUS REVENUE
In accounting terms, income and revenue are two different concepts. Revenue is the "top line" amount, the amount generated from all of a company's activity. Income, on the other hand, is the "bottom line" amount, the amount that is left after all expenses have been deducted from revenue. In other words, revenue minus expenses equals income.

INCOME STATEMENT

The income statement is also known as the profit and loss statement (P&L). This statement tracks a company's profit and loss over *a period of time*. We will cover the P&L in greater detail in the next chapter.

The basic format for the income statement is:

	sales revenue
–	cost of goods sold
	gross profit
–	operating expenses
	income from operations
+/–	non-operating items
	gross income
–	taxes
	net income

STATEMENT OF RETAINED EARNINGS

This financial statement shows the changes in an owner's equity in a company over a set period of time. The statement of retained earnings will highlight the owner's equity position at both the beginning and the ending of the reporting period. The statement of retained earnings includes information on the beginning retained earnings, the net income, and the dividends paid during the period.

The format for a statement of retained earnings is:

beginning balance, retained earnings
+ net income
– dividends

ending balance, retained earnings

Let's look at an example of a statement of retained earnings.

ELEGANT INTERIORS, LLC
Statement of Retained Earnings
For the Year Ending December 31, 2008

Retained Earnings—January 1, 2008	**$200,000**
Plus: Net Income	+ 75,000
	$ 275,000
Less: Dividends	– 20,000
Retained Earnings—December 31, 2008	**$255,000**

STATEMENT OF CASH FLOW

The statement of cash flow tracks a company's cash flow from operations, financing (i.e., loans), and investments *over a given period*. Essentially, it shows how money has flowed into and out of the company. By reviewing the statement of cash flow, you can determine a company's short-term liquidity. Liquidity is important because it is the ability to convert an asset to cash, both quickly and cheaply (without incurring extra expenses or having to provide a discount).

A company's cash flow is tracked by looking at the three ways it enters and leaves the company: operating activities, investing activities, and financing activities. The operating activities or operations section of the statement of cash flow analyzes a company's cash flow from net income or losses. The next section of the statement analyzes a company's cash flow from investing activities, which can include the purchases or sales of long-term assets (property, for example) and the purchases or sales of investment securities. The last part of the statement shows cash flow from financing activities, such as taking out or paying back a loan, sale and purchase of stock, and paying dividends.

The bottom line of the statement of cash flow will show the net increase or decrease in cash for the period.

MEMO

RE: FINANCIAL STATEMENT TERMS

When you read a financial statement, you may be overwhelmed by the number of unfamiliar terms. Here is a brief rundown of some of the common terms used on financial statements:

- *amortization*—reduction in value of intangible assets; for example, donations to charitable causes
- *asset*—anything that a business can lay claim to; for example, a building, a vehicle, inventory, cash, and even patents and goodwill
- *cost of goods sold (COGS)*—the expenses for materials and production of products sold
- *depreciation*—the reduction in value of a tangible asset over the course of its useful life
- *EBIT*—an abbreviation for earnings before interest and taxes
- *equity*—the residual value of ownership shown on the balance sheet; will always equal "total assets" minus "total liabilities"
- *net income*—the earnings of a company after satisfying all costs, expenses, and tax obligations
- *sales*—the revenue from products or services sold
- *total assets*—the sum of current assets (such as cash) and noncurrent assets (fixed assets such as buildings and intangible assets such as goodwill)
- *total debt*—the combined amount of current liabilities and long-term liabilities; also referred to as "total liabilities"

Here is an example of a statement of cash flow.

CARPET SUPERCENTER
Statement of Cash Flow
For the Year Ending December 31, 2008

Cash Flow from Operations	
Net Income	$2,787,000
Changes in Accounts Receivable	(226,000)
Changes in Liabilities	965,000
Changes in Inventories	(431,000)
Changes in Other Operating Activities	(25,000)
Total Cash from Operations	3,070,000
Cash Flow from Investing Activities	
Capital Expenditures	(3,928,000)
Investments	(827,000)
Other Cash Flows from Investing Activities	62,000
Total Cash from Investing Activities	(4,693,000)
Cash Flow from Financing Activities	
Dividends Paid	(380,000)
Sales/Purchases of Stock	(720,000)
Net Borrowings	101,000
Other Cash Flows from Financing Activities	(5,000)
Total Cash from Financing Activities	(1,004,000)
Change in Cash and Cash Equivalents	($2,627,000)

FINANCIAL STATEMENT RATIOS AND CALCULATIONS

There are many ratios and calculations that are used in financial statements. We'll go over these and demonstrate how you can perform the calculations on your own. This will help you to gain a better understanding of the information that is analyzed and conveyed in the financial statements.

Debt-to-Equity Ratio

The debt-to-equity ratio compares a company's total debt to owners' or shareholders' equity. From this ratio, you can see the proportion of a company's assets that is provided by creditors and the proportion that is provided by owners. In general, the higher the ratio of debt to equity, the less solvent the company is likely to be over the long term. These numbers are found on the balance sheet. To calculate the debt-to-equity ratio, use this formula:

debt-to-equity ratio = total liabilities (or debt) ÷ owners' equity

Basic Earning Power Ratio

The basic earning power ratio isolates earnings from uses of leverage and taxes, allowing you to more accurately and directly compare a company to others that use a different approach to financing or have different tax situations. You can find this ratio by dividing a company's earnings before interest and taxes (EBIT) by the total assets. The EBIT, which is net income plus interest plus taxes, is found on the income statement, and the total assets would be on the balance sheet. Here is the formula for calculating basic earning power:

basic earning power = EBIT ÷ total assets

Earnings per Share

The earnings per share figure shows how much profit a company earns for every share of common stock outstanding. Common stock shares represent ownership in a company. The earnings per share figure is calculated by dividing the net income by the number of shares of common stock that are outstanding. In general, a ratio that increases from one period to the next is an indication of strong company growth, because it shows that the company's earnings for each share of stock have increased. The formula is:

earnings per share = net income ÷ number of shares of common stock outstanding

Gross Profit Ratio

The gross profit ratio shows the amount of each sales dollar that is available to pay expenses. To calculate the gross profit ratio, you need the sales and cost of goods sold amounts from the income statement. The higher the gross profit ratio, the more easily a company can cover expenses from sales. The formula to calculate this ratio is:

gross profit ratio = (sales – cost of goods sold) ÷ sales

Profit Margin Ratio

The profit margin ratio shows how profitable a company's sales are. The higher the ratio, the more profit earned from each dollar in sales. Profit margin is calculated by dividing the net income by the sales. These are both found on the income statement. Here is the formula:

profit margin ratio = net income ÷ sales

Return on Assets

Return on assets (ROA) shows the after-tax profit as a percentage of total assets. In general, the higher the ratio, the greater the profit from the company's assets. To calculate this ratio, you need the net income from the income statement and the total assets from the balance sheet. The formula is:

return on assets = net income ÷ total assets

Return on Equity

Return on equity shows income as a percentage of equity. It is a measure of profitability where the higher the ratio, the more profit earned by the owners. You need the net income from the income statement and the owners' equity from the balance sheet to calculate this ratio. Here is the formula:

return on equity ratio = net income ÷ equity

UNDERSTANDING INVENTORY

Companies can use one of three different methods to calculate the value of inventory. Because inventory is captured as an asset in the financial statements, it will be good for you to have a basic understanding of the concepts of inventory valuation. The three methods are the average cost method, the first in, first out (FIFO) method, and the last in, first out (LIFO) method.

Average Cost Method

The average cost method of valuing inventory assumes that the inventory consists of non-unique items. In other words, it assumes that each item is similar to every other item. It uses the average unit cost to calculate the value of the current inventory. The formula for the average cost method is:

inventory value = average unit cost × total quantity of units in current inventory

If you don't know the average unit cost, you can get it using this formula:

average unit cost = total unit cost ÷ total quantity of units in current inventory

The benefit to using the average cost method is that it will generally even out price fluctuations over time.

FIFO Method

The first in, first out (FIFO) method is actually the most common and preferred method of inventory valuation and the one you are most likely to hear about if you work in a company that stocks inventory.

As with the average cost method, FIFO assumes an inventory of non-unique goods. It also assumes that inventory is sold in the order in which it is stocked—oldest items sold first and newest items sold last. Thus, first in, first out.

The calculation for valuing inventory using FIFO is a little more difficult than the average cost method. To do so, you need the unit cost per batch of items and then you need to count the inventory back from the newest batch. So, you must perform a specific calculation for each batch of items that you stock.

First, you would find the unit cost per batch using this formula:

unit cost per batch = cost ÷ quantity in batch

Find this cost for each batch. Then, calculate the inventory value of each batch:

inventory value = unit cost × quantity in inventory

Find the inventory value of each batch and add the values together, counting backward from the newest batch.

Let's work through an example. Suppose you work for a snack company and your division produces Tempting Treats. You need to value the inventory of Tempting Treats based on three batches. First, you need to know the cost and quantity for each batch:

first batch: cost = $27,888; quantity = 40,005
second batch: cost = $23,720; quantity = 30,202
third batch: cost = $22,695; quantity = 30,155

You also need to know how much inventory you have. We'll say there are 38,005 units in inventory.

So, for each batch, you can now find the unit cost, using the formula from before:

unit cost per batch = cost ÷ quantity in batch

first batch = $27,888 ÷ 40,005
= $0.697

second batch = $23,720 ÷ 30,202
= $0.785

third batch = $22,695 ÷ 30,155
= $0.753

To get the inventory value, you multiply the unit cost for each batch by the amount of inventory left from that batch. Because you are using FIFO, you count backward from the third batch (the newest batch) to fill in the inventory. It looks like this:

$$\text{third batch (the newest batch)} = \$0.753 \times 30{,}155 = \$22{,}706.72$$

Because your total inventory is 38,005, you subtract the third batch quantity from that number to find the quantity still in inventory from the second batch:

$$38{,}005 - 30{,}155 = 7{,}850$$

That becomes the quantity that you will use to value the inventory from the second batch:

$$\text{second batch} = \$0.785 \times 7{,}850 = \$6{,}162.25$$

You have then accounted for all of the inventory, so you know that there is nothing left in inventory from the first batch:

$$\text{first batch (the oldest batch)} = \$0.697 \times 0 = \$0$$

Add the batch values together to get the inventory valuation:

$$\$0 + \$6{,}162.25 + \$22{,}706.72 = \$28{,}868.97$$

LIFO Method

The last in, first out (LIFO) method is a highly regulated method for valuing inventory in part because it allows companies to report lower profits during periods when costs have increased, which in turn allows the companies to pay lower taxes. However, you won't run across this method all that often. In fact, fewer than 10% of publicly traded companies use this method. Like the other two, it assumes an inventory of non-unique items. Unlike FIFO, though, it assumes that the newest inventory is sold first with the oldest items sold last. To calculate the inventory value using LIFO, you would use the unit cost per batch of items and then count forward from the oldest batch.

The formulas for LIFO are the same as for FIFO. First find the unit cost per batch:

$$\text{unit cost per batch} = \text{cost} \div \text{quantity in batch}$$

Then, calculate the inventory value of each batch:

$$\text{inventory value} = \text{unit cost} \times \text{quantity in inventory}$$

Here is the difference between LIFO and FIFO. After finding the value for each batch and adding the values together, you count *forward* from the oldest batch.

Let's look at the example we used for FIFO and apply the LIFO method to it. Because we already calculated the unit cost for each batch under the FIFO method, we can state that we know the following:

first batch: cost = $27,888; quantity = 40,005; unit cost = $0.697
second batch: cost = $23,720; quantity = 30,202; unit cost = $0.785
third batch: cost = $22,695; quantity = 30,155; unit cost = $0.753

We also know that there are 38,005 units left in inventory. So, to get the inventory value, we count forward from the oldest batch, the first batch. Because the first batch total quantity was 40,005 units, the entire remaining inventory of 38,005 units is in that batch.

$$\text{first batch (the oldest batch)} = \$0.697 \times 38{,}005$$
$$= \$26{,}489.49$$

None of the inventory is from the second and third batches:

$$\text{second batch} = \$0.785 \times 0$$
$$= \$0$$

$$\text{third batch (the newest batch)} = \$0.753 \times 0$$
$$= \$0$$

In this scenario, the inventory value is $26,489.49.

As you can see, using LIFO versus FIFO makes a difference in the value of the inventory.

INVENTORY RATES AND A RATIO

There are two rates and a ratio that you can use to analyze a company's inventory levels: inventory turnover rate at cost, inventory turnover rate at retail, and inventory turnover ratio. These show how quickly (or slowly) a company sells its inventory. Once you have this information, you can compare a company's current rate to rates of past periods and to its competitor's or a similar company's rates. In general, a high turnover rate is preferable because it means a company's inventory is selling well. However, a turnover rate that is too high or too low could be a bad thing, depending on the industry and depending on how the current rate compares with rates from past periods.

Inventory Turnover Rate at Cost

The inventory turnover rate at cost measures the inventory turnover rate over a period of time, with set start and end dates. This is the method by which inventory turnover is generally calculated, because inventory is valued at cost, not by retail sale price. To calculate the inventory turnover rate at cost, you need to know the cost of goods sold, the starting inventory value at cost, and the ending value at cost.

First, find the average inventory value at cost using this formula:

average inventory value at cost = (starting inventory value at cost + ending inventory value at cost) ÷ 2

Once you have the average value, you can find the rate. Use this formula:

inventory turnover rate = cost of goods sold ÷ average inventory value at cost

Inventory Turnover Rate at Retail

Inventory turnover rate at retail also measures turnover over a period time. Instead of using cost of goods sold, though, you will use the net sales. Using this rate allows you to see the inventory turnover rate based on the same method that sales are recorded (because sales are recorded based on the retail price, not the cost). So, the formulas to find this rate are very similar to those for finding inventory turnover rate at cost.

First, find the average inventory value at retail using this formula:

average inventory value at retail = (starting inventory value at retail + ending inventory value at retail) ÷ 2

Then use the average value to find the rate. The formula is:

inventory turnover rate = net sales ÷ average inventory value at retail

Inventory Turnover Ratio

The inventory turnover ratio can help you to understand a company's liquidity. The ratio shows the company's ability to convert inventory into cash. In general, the higher the ratio, the more potentially liquid a company is. To calculate this ratio, you need the sales from the income statement and the inventory value from the balance sheet.

Here is the formula for calculating the inventory turnover ratio:

inventory turnover ratio = sales ÷ inventory value

Now that you have an understanding of the various types and components of financial statements, we'll move on to look at the income statement or P&L in greater detail in the next chapter.

CHAPTER NINE

The Income Statement/Profit and Loss Statement

The income statement is a financial statement of many names. It is known as the statement of income, statement of earnings, statement of operations, statement of operating results, or the profit and loss (P&L) statement. Phew! That's a lot of names for one statement. In this chapter, we refer to it as the income statement or the P&L.

MEMO
RE: TIME PERIOD FOR A P&L
Pay attention to the time period for your P&L. Unlike a balance sheet, which is a snapshot of a company's finances at a particular date in time, the P&L shows a listing of what has transpired or happened during a particular period in time.

The P&L summarizes the revenues, costs, and expenses incurred during a specific period, usually a month, a quarter, or a year. It follows a fairly standard format that starts off with the revenue (sales) and subtracts the expenses, such as cost of goods sold, operating expenses, and so on. The bottom line is the net profit. A regularly prepared—and monitored—P&L statement not only provides a company with important information about revenues and expenses, but it also identifies places in the business where changes might be necessary to decrease expenses.

This chapter will walk you through the preparation of a P&L statement.

SAMPLE PROFIT AND LOSS STATEMENT

Here is one sample of what a P&L looks like:

AQUATIC ADVENTURES, INC.
P&L Statement
January–March 2008

Q1 2008 Profit and Loss	*Jan.*	*Feb.*	*Mar.*	*YTD*
Net Sales	**$132,850.00**	**$140,250.00**	**$156,342.00**	***$429,442.00***
Direct Costs of Goods	$28,572.00	$29,300.00	$30,455.00	*$88,327.00*
Other Costs of Goods	$250.00	$400.00	$450.00	*$1,100.00*
Cost of Goods Sold	$28,822.00	$29,700.00	$30,905.00	*$89,427.00*
Gross Margin	**$104,028.00**	**$110,550.00**	**$125,437.00**	***$340,015.00***
SG&A Expenses				
Payroll	$52,000.00	$52,000.00	$57,200.00	*$161,200.00*
Depreciation	$13,450.00	$13,450.00	$13,450.00	*$40,350.00*
Advertising	$0.00	$5,000.00	$7,500.00	*$12,500.00*
Rent	$16,000.00	$16,000.00	$16,000.00	*$48,000.00*
Insurance	$4,000.00	$4,000.00	$4,000.00	*$12,000.00*
Payroll Taxes	$5,500.00	$5,500.00	$5,500.00	*$16,500.00*
Other	$3,023.00	$2,790.00	$3,588.00	*$9,401.00*
Total SG&A Expenses	**$93,973.00**	**$98,740.00**	**$107,238.00**	***$299,951.00***
Profit before Interest and Taxes	$10,055.00	$11,810.00	$18,199.00	*$40,064.00*
Interest Expense	$590.00	$590.00	$590.00	*$1,770.00*
Taxes Incurred	$0.00	$0.00	$0.00	*$0.00*
Net Profit	**$9,465.00**	**$11,220.00**	**$17,609.00**	***$38,294.00***
Approx. Net Profit/Sales	**7%**	**8%**	**11%**	***9%***

This P&L measures the profit and loss for the first three months of the year and rolls them all up into a year-to-date (YTD) column.

PREPARING A P&L STATEMENT

Here, in a few simple steps, is an overview of how to create a P&L statement. You will want to use Microsoft Excel or a similar program to prepare a P&L statement.

Step 1: Set Up the Statement, Paying Attention to the Heading

The heading of a P&L is important to its usability. A reader should be able to clearly identify the company (and division or department, if applicable) that the P&L has been prepared for, along with the period of time that is being examined. To show the time period that is being examined, write it out by its ending date: "For the Year Ending December 31, 2008," for example.

Step 2: Gather Your Data and Enter the Corresponding Amounts in Your Spreadsheet

In order to create a P&L, you must know:

- net sales
- cost of goods sold
- selling, general, and administrative (SG&A) expenses
- other income and other expenses

Let's take a look at each of these items.

Net Sales

Net sales indicates the total sales during the time period being examined for the P&L less allowances for any returns and discounts. Net sales is the top-line amount, and it is where the income process begins. The amount that is allowed for returns varies from business to business. Large companies tend to have larger returns, as do retail businesses that have lenient return policies. The return allowance is generally figured as a percentage of total sales. The discount allowance shows the difference between the standard (or list or catalog) price and the actual price paid by customers. This allowance will decrease total sales to reflect the prices that are actually paid.

Cost of Goods Sold

Cost of goods sold (COGS) is also known as cost of sales. For retailers and wholesalers, it is the total price paid for the products sold during the period being examined (raw materials and labor costs, for example). Essentially, it is the purchase cost of merchandise used for resale. Cost of goods sold does not include any selling or administrative expenses. For service and professional companies, there are no costs of goods sold. Instead, these companies will have the costs to generate sales of their services included in other sections of their P&Ls.

Manufacturer's Cost of Goods Sold

The method for calculating the cost of goods sold for manufacturers is different from the method for retailers and wholesalers, because manufacturers' costs of goods sold are divided into two categories: direct costs and indirect costs. Direct costs include inventory costs, which are calculated the same way as for retailers and wholesalers, along with raw material and direct labor costs. Direct labor costs are the costs to convert the raw materials into the finished product.

Indirect costs include any indirect labor, factory overhead, and materials and supplies. Indirect labor differs from direct labor in that it includes costs that aren't involved in converting the raw materials into the finished products. For example, indirect labor costs would include shipping personnel and office managers. Factory overhead includes depreciation of plant and equipment, factory utilities, real estate taxes, and any other factory personnel who do not work directly to create the products. Materials and supplies are those items that are not used in the actual manufacturing process (those that are used in the manufacturing process are included in the direct costs).

As with retailers and wholesalers, the costs of goods sold for manufacturers do not include any selling or administrative costs.

MEMO

RE: SELLING, GENERAL, AND ADMINISTRATIVE EXPENSES

The selling, general, and administrative (SG&A) category contains fixed, variable, and discretionary expenses and may include:

- salaried personnel
- travel and entertainment
- rent
- utilities
- postage
- printing
- insurance
- interest
- depreciation
- dues/subscriptions
- advertising

Selling, General, and Administrative Expenses

Companies, whether they are manufacturers, retailers, or wholesalers, record two types of expenses on the P&L: selling expenses and general and administrative expenses.

Selling expenses are the direct and indirect expenses incurred while making sales. Such expenses include sales team salaries, commissions, advertising, warehousing, and shipping. General and administrative expenses are operating expenses that do not deal with sales. Such expenses include nonsales salaries, supplies, overhead like rent and utilities, travel, and so on. These expenses differ from costs that are included in the cost of goods sold in that they are not directly related to the production or acquisition of the item that is being sold.

Other Income and Other Expenses

This sounds a bit like a catchall term, doesn't it? However, you can't put just anything in this category. Rather, "Other Income" is defined as income that is not directly related to business operations. It includes interest, dividends, rents, royalties, capital gains, and any miscellaneous sales. "Other Expenses" is defined as unexpected losses that are not directly related to the normal course of business. "Other Income" is added to net operating profit and "Other Expenses" is subtracted from it to get the net profit before taxes.

Here is another sample of a P&L. In this example, the company is looking at a period of one fiscal year (FY) and comparing it to the prior year.

GLOWING GLASSWARE
P&L Statement
FY 2007 and FY 2008

	2007	*2008*
Net Sales	1,500,000	2,000,000
Cost of Sales	(350,000)	(375,000)
Gross Margin	**1,150,000**	**1,625,000**
Operating Expenses (SG&A)	(235,000)	(260,000)
Operating Income	**915,000**	**1,365,000**
Other Income (Expense)	40,000	60,000
Extraordinary Gain (Loss)	—	(15,000)
Interest Expense	(50,000)	(50,000)
Net Profit before Taxes (Pretax Income)	**905,000**	**1,360,000**
Taxes	(300,000)	(475,000)
Net Income	**605,000**	**885,000**

Step 3: Calculate Gross Margin

Gross margin may also be referred to as the gross profit. You can calculate the gross margin for the period after you have entered in the net sales and cost of goods sold. The basic formula for gross margin is:

gross margin = net sales – cost of goods sold

Step 4: Calculate the Net Operating Profit

Net operating profit is also called the operating income. It is the difference between the gross margin and the selling, general, and administrative expenses:

net operating profit = gross margin – SG&A expenses

Step 5: Calculate the Net Profit before Taxes

This is where you add "Other Income" and subtract "Other Expenses." These are added to or subtracted from the net operating profit (or operating income) to calculate the net profit before taxes.

Step 6: Calculate Net Profit

Here it is: the bottom line! Let's hope it is a positive number.

To calculate the net profit, subtract any taxes, such as state or federal income taxes, from the net profit before taxes line. The result is one of the key indicators for a company: the net profit or loss.

The sample P&L on the facing page looks at a full year of revenue and expenses broken out by month. It just shows another way that you can set up your P&L statement.

PRACTICE P&L

We've included a blank P&L template for you to practice with (see last page of chapter). This template has some common line items included so you can look up those items for your company or department and enter them into the practice sheet. This will give you an opportunity to see how readily available the information is. It will also give you a good idea of the financial health of your company or department!

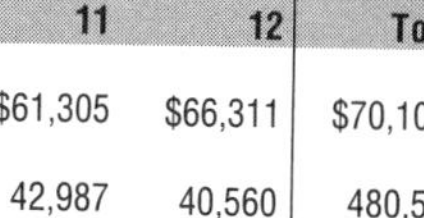

PROFIT AND LOSS SAMPLE

Month	1	2	3	4	5	6	7	8	9	10	11	12	Total
Revenue	$55,007	$54,992	$56,888	$56,897	$57,993	$59,030	$56,444	$59,577	$59,398	$57,222	$61,305	$66,311	$70,1064
Cost of sales	34,511	36,723	38,978	42,210	43,738	38,949	40,121	41,999	40,566	39,222	42,987	40,560	480,564
Gross profit	20,496	18,269	17,910	14,687	14,255	20,081	16,323	17,578	18,832	18,000	18,318	25,751	220,500
Gross profit margin (%)	37.3%	33.2%	31.5%	25.8%	24.6%	34.0%	28.9%	29.5%	31.7%	31.5%	29.9%	38.8%	31.5%
Selling, General, & Administrative Expenses													
Rent	1,300	1,300	1,300	1,300	1,300	1,300	1,300	1,300	1,300	1,300	1,300	1,300	15,600
Power (light, heat, electricity, gas)	650	650	650	650	650	650	650	650	650	650	650	650	7,800
Telephone	490	435	467	455	498	415	472	453	480	479	499	452	5,595
Insurance	900	900	900	900	900	900	900	900	900	900	900	900	10,800
Postage	150	150	150	150	150	150	150	150	150	150	150	150	1,800
Advertising	2,000	0	0	0	0	0	0	0	2,500	3,000	3,500	2,500	13,500
Interest and bank charges payable	130	130	130	130	130	130	130	130	130	130	130	130	1,560
Stationery	0	0	0	0	0	3,750	0	0	0	0	0	0	3,750
Salaries	8,020	8,020	8,020	8,020	8,020	8,700	8,700	8,700	8,700	8,700	8,700	8,700	101,000
Equipment	0	0	0	0	0	0	0	0	0	0	0	0	0
Legal/professional fees	300	300	300	300	300	300	300	300	300	300	300	300	3,600
Depreciation	1,235	1,235	1,235	1,235	1,235	1,235	1,235	1,235	1,235	1,235	1,235	1,235	14,820
Other specific expenses	200	200	200	200	200	200	200	200	200	200	200	200	2,400
Total SG&A	15,375	13,320	13,352	13,340	13,383	17,730	14,037	14,018	16,545	17,044	17,564	16,517	182,225
Net profit	5,121	4,949	4,558	1,347	872	2,351	2,286	3,560	2,287	956	754	9,234	38,275
Net profit margin	9.3%	9.0%	8.0%	2.4%	1.5%	4.0%	4.1%	6.0%	3.9%	1.7%	1.2%	13.9%	5.5%

PROFIT and LOSS Statement
For the Year Ending December 31, 2008

	Jan	Feb	Mar	Apr	May	Jun	Jul	Aug	Sep	Oct	Nov	Dec
Revenue:												
Gross Sales												
Less: Returns/Allowances												
Net Sales	0	0	0	0	0	0	0	0	0	0	0	0
Cost of Goods:												
Materials												
Variable Labor												
Misc.												
	0	0	0	0	0	0	0	0	0	0	0	0
Less: Ending Inventory												
Cost of Goods Sold	0	0	0	0	0	0	0	0	0	0	0	0
Gross Profit (Loss)	0	0	0	0	0	0	0	0	0	0	0	0
Controllable Expenses:												
Advertising												
Payroll												
Payroll Taxes and Benefits												
Sales Commissions												
Professional Fees												
Operating Supplies												
Travel												
Communications												
Maintenance and Repairs												
Office Supplies												
Miscellaneous												
Fixed Expenses:												
Interest												
Depreciation												
Property Taxes												
Rent												
Insurance												
Utilities												
Bad Debts												
Bank Service Charges												
Amortization												
Total Expenses	0	0	0	0	0	0	0	0	0	0	0	0
Net Operating Income	0	0	0	0	0	0	0	0	0	0	0	0
Other Income:												
Gain (Loss) on Sale of Assets												
Interest Income												
Total Other Income	0	0	0	0	0	0	0	0	0	0	0	0
Net Income (Loss)	0	0	0	0	0	0	0	0	0	0	0	0
Taxes												
Net Income (Loss) after taxes	0	0	0	0	0	0	0	0	0	0	0	0

CHAPTER TEN

Budgeting Process

Feeling beleaguered by budgets? Then this chapter is for you!

If you were to listen to the many common complaints, you would think that budgets exist solely to be cut. It is not so. The purpose of a budget is to show you where your money is coming from and where it is going. A budget as a financial plan and a thoughtfully prepared one will help keep companies, departments, and projects on track. Budgets usually cover a specific budget period, most often 12 months, but the period can be shorter or longer, such as a budget for a specific project, for example.

A budget is a plan to:

- manage finances
- ensure your company can fund current commitments and meet objectives
- support financial decisions
- ensure your company has enough money for future growth—new projects, new team members, and so on.

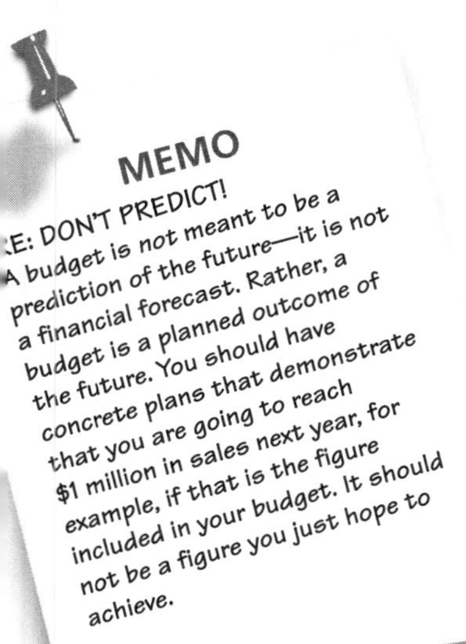

Regardless of your profession, at some point in your career you will most likely have to work with a budget, so it will be to your benefit to get over any sense of intimidation that you may have. This chapter will guide you through the process of establishing a budget so you will feel confident when involved in budget discussions and you will be able to create your own budgets when you need to do so.

WHERE THE BUDGET FITS

A budget is a component of business planning and should be included in a company's overall business plan. Business planning is the cycle of looking at a business and analyzing performance so changes can be made in the near term, if necessary, to ensure that the business moves in a positive direction. A business plan is a road map for a company. It sets out the strategy that a company will use in the upcoming period to achieve success. As we stated, a budget exists to show where money is coming from and where it is going, which is an essential part of the business plan.

An annual business plan should include:

- the company's goals and objectives for the year
- changes that a company wants to make in the upcoming year
- known or potential changes in the marketplace, with customers or with competitors
- key performance indicators
- any operational changes
- any issues or problems
- information about human resources—the management team and other personnel
- financial performance and projections or forecasts
- details about investment in the business (if any)

A business planning cycle should not stop when the annual business plan has been printed and handed out to all the team members. The cycle is meant to be fluid and is most successful when it is an ongoing process. A typical business planning cycle looks like this:

- Review current performance against prior year-to-date and current-year targets.
- Identify opportunities and threats.
- Analyze successes and failures.
- Review key objectives and modify your longer-term planning, if necessary.
- Identify the resource implication of this review and build a budget.
- Define the new year's P&L and balance sheet targets.
- Conclude the plan.
- Review it regularly!

CREATING A BUDGET

Your goal in preparing a budget should be to make it as realistic as possible. A realistic budget is one that uses historical information along with projections about the future state of the company, such as changes in the competitive environment, rising production costs, or a potential realignment of resources.

One of the keys to creating a realistic budget is to invest the time needed to make sure the budget is comprehensive. Another key is to involve the right people, who also need to commit to an investment in time. Who are the right people? Well, that will depend on your company and industry. Generally, however, you should at least involve members of the financial team, who can provide you with information for overhead and other costs, and sales and marketing team members, who can provide you with projected sales and information on marketplace trends.

Do not try to bang out a budget in one afternoon. Set up a series of meetings with key people and discuss goals, projected expenses, the marketplace, changes in production costs, and whatever other topics will affect your budget. Consider the historical data that you have compiled. Then, balance all of your information to create a detailed, comprehensive and well-thought-out budget.

There are many resources available to help you prepare a budget, including software packages. Using Excel or some other software will streamline the actual work of creating the budget document. But if you are an old-fashioned type, you can write out your budget with pencil and paper. The point is not to let the budget process overwhelm you. Approach it the way you feel comfortable, and it will be an easier process for everyone involved.

Whatever system you use for creating your budget, it is very important that you check your math throughout the process. If you are using Excel or a similar spreadsheet, double-check your formulas and make sure that all mathematical operations are properly executed.

MEMO

RE: USING FORMULAS IN EXCEL

Just as you would when performing calculations, Excel follows an order of operations when calculating a formula. It starts with items in parentheses, then moves on to exponents, multiplication, division, and, last, addition and subtraction. You can enter formulas in an Excel worksheet manually either by typing the formula starting with the equal (=) sign or by typing in the equal sign, clicking on the cell, typing in the operation, and then clicking on the next cell.

To edit formulas, you can double-click on the cell and then either press F2 while the cell is selected or click on the formula bar while the cell is selected.

The main formula errors in Excel are:

- #DIV/0!—The formula is attempting to divide by zero (which can't be done).
- ##NAME?—The name used in the formula is not recognized.
- ##REF!—The formula refers to a cell that is not valid (it may have been deleted or it may not contain the right type of value).

TYPES OF BUDGETS

There are three main types of budgets: operating budgets, capital budgets, and cash budgets.

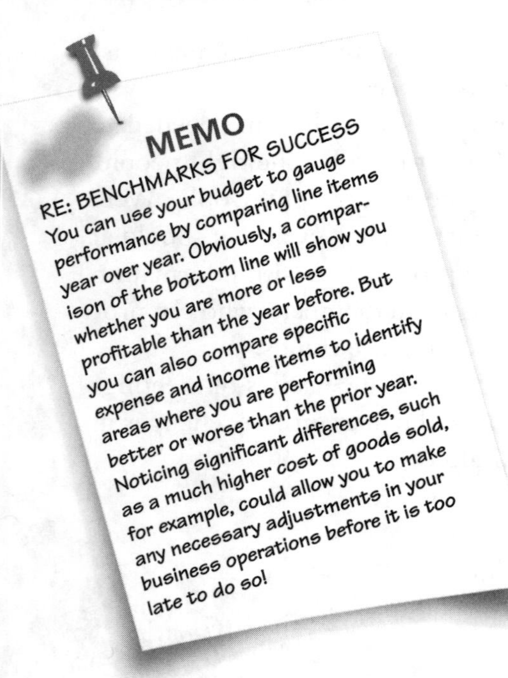

Operating Budgets

Operating budgets consist of three parts: the statistical budget, the expense budget, and the revenue budget. The statistical budget is a projection of business activity for the year. This would include the number of contracts to be signed, sales estimates, number of units to be produced, and so on. The expense budget is a projection of all costs involved in operating the business for the year. The revenue budget is a projection of the income for the year. These three combine in the operating budget.

Capital Budgets

Capital budgets are used to account for potential expenditures for major fixed equipment (for example, a building, a boiler, a new roof, etc.) and major movable equipment (copy machines, computers, and so forth).

Cash Budgets

A cash budget is usually prepared last in the budgeting process and consists of estimates of the business's cash needs for the year, as compared with projections of the cash receipts for the year.

MEMO

RE: FIXED COSTS AND OVERHEAD

Here are some examples of the types of expenses for fixed costs or overhead:

- staff costs—salaries, benefits
- rent or mortgage
- utilities—heating, lighting, phone
- vehicle expenses
- equipment costs
- advertising and promotion
- postage
- supplies
- legal and professional fees
- travel expenses

CALCULATING RENT OR MORTGAGE

When preparing a budget, you will need to include rent or mortgage payments in your fixed costs. If your company owns the building where its office is located, then you will only have to look at the mortgage payments (if any) and multiply them by the number of months in your budget.

If your company leases office space, however, you will have to look at the lease before being able to calculate the total expense. This should tell you whether the rent is gross or net. With gross rent, the landlord pays for the building operating expenses, such as heat, electricity, water, maintenance, and taxes. These are also fixed costs, so it is important that you know whether they are included or if you need to break them out separately. Net rent, on the other hand, is where the tenant pays all the building operating expenses.

Once you know what type of rent your company has, you can calculate it for the budget period. For example, if the rent is $1,700 per month, you would multiply $1,700 by 12 to get the annual rent of $20,400. If the rent is net, you would add on the building operating expenses.

SAMPLE SIMPLE BUDGET

Some companies will find that simple budgets meet their needs. Here is a sample of a very simple marketing department budget. It accounts for expenses for a full year rather than breaking them out by month.

MARKETING DEPARTMENT BUDGET
January 1, 2009–December 31, 2009

	Actual	*Budget*	*Difference*
Advertising	$142,000	$155,000	$13,000
Catalogs	27,800	27,800	—
Website	7,550	7,550	—
Promotions	42,500	42,000	(500)
Trade Shows	81,900	80,000	(1,900)
Brochures	13,600	14,200	600
Other	650	500	(150)
Total Marketing Expense	**$316,000**	**$327,050**	**$11,050**

A budget is critical to the financial success of a business. It doesn't need to be complicated, but it does need to be prepared thoughtfully with input from the key players in your company. A good budget will keep you on the path to success!

CHAPTER ELEVEN

Basic Accounting Methods

Accounting is the process of recording, classifying, reporting, and analyzing financial data. This information is summarized in reports and statements. That sounds simple enough, right? But you know that there is a lot more to accounting than just the preparation of a few reports. This chapter will give you a taste of accounting. We won't attempt to teach you everything you'd need to know to become an accountant, but we will attempt to provide you with an overview of the most common accounting methods and standards.

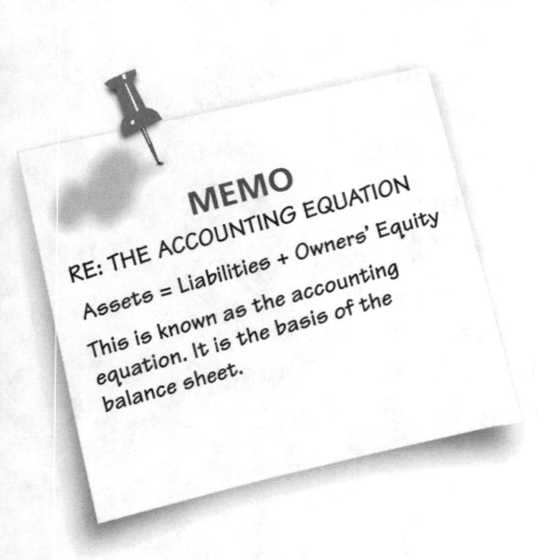

There are two primary methods of accounting that we will cover in this chapter: accrual accounting and cash accounting. These are also referred to as accrual basis and cost basis accounting and as accrual method and cost method accounting. We'll look at how the two differ and some basics to using each.

ACCRUAL ACCOUNTING

First, let's look at accrual accounting. This is the method that is standard accounting practice for most companies. Using the accrual method of accounting, a company counts transactions when the sale is made, the order is placed, the product is delivered, or the service occurs, regardless of when the money is actually paid or received. Simply put, a company registers transactions as events occur. If a company makes a sale, the income is counted at that time, whether or not the purchaser has paid. Similarly, if a company has made a purchase, the expenses are counted at the time the company receives the goods or services, whether or not it has paid for them yet.

The trick with accrual accounting is knowing when to record a sale or purchase. Sales or purchases are recorded only when they are complete; they don't go on the books at the start of a job, but when the job is finished. For example, if your company made a sale of 10,000 rocking chairs and you delivered them in increments of 1,000, you would not record the sale until all 10,000 were shipped and delivered.

Companies that stock an inventory of items to be sold are required by the IRS to use accrual accounting.

MEMO

RE: TAX DEDUCTIONS

Whether a company uses accrual accounting or cash accounting affects how income and expenses are counted for tax deductions. Using accrual accounting, expenses are claimed in the year in which they are incurred—even if they haven't been paid yet. Using cash accounting, by contrast, expenses are claimed only when they are actually paid.

CASH ACCOUNTING

Companies that use the cash accounting method record income when the money is received and record expenses when they are paid. This is in contrast to the accrual accounting method.

Here is an example of how accrual and cash accounting differ. Let's say you work for a website developer. Your team completed the development of a new website and invoiced for the work in November. The company for which you built the website does not pay the invoice until January. Under the accrual accounting method, you would record the income in November. Under the cash accounting method, you would record the payment when you receive it: in January.

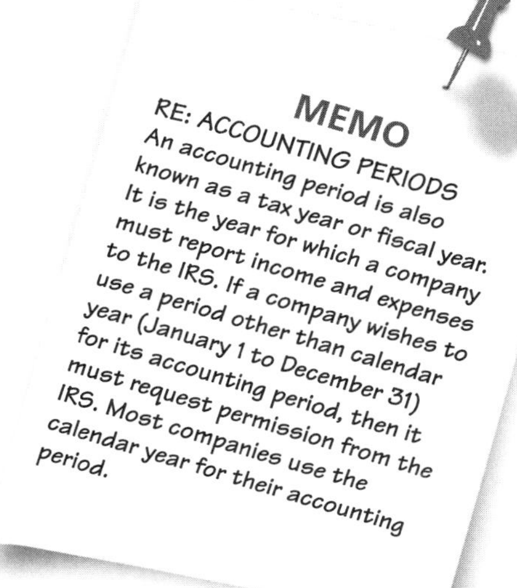

Now we'll look at an expense for the website development firm. Suppose the firm purchased a new server in April, on credit. The payment for the server was made in May. Under the accrual accounting method, the expense would be recorded in April, when the server was purchased and you were obligated to pay for it. Under the cash accounting method, however, the expense would not be recorded until May, when it was actually paid.

ACCOUNTING CYCLE

The accounting cycle refers to the steps that are repeated for every accounting period. The accounting cycle starts with accounting entries for each transaction and ends with closing the books. Take a look at the process even if you are sure you will never have anything to do with the accounting of your company. Knowing the process that occurs for each accounting period will likely open your eyes to, among other things, why records are kept the way they are and the importance of providing backup for expenses.

These are the steps that comprise the accounting cycle. First, there are four steps that are taken as each transaction occurs:

1. *Identify the transaction through an original source.* Original sources include invoices, receipts, purchase orders, deposit slips, and the like. They should include information about the transaction such as the date, the amount, and a description of the business purpose.
2. *Analyze the transaction.* Analysis includes determining the accounts that are affected by the transaction and which one will be credited and which one will be debited. For example, if a company made a sale of $1,500 to a customer that was billed for the entire amount, the transaction could be entered as a $1,500 credit in the revenue account and $1,500 debit in the accounts receivable account.
3. *Make journal entries.* Transactions enter the accounting system through journal entries. A journal entry is a record of each transaction, and it includes an explanation of the transaction, which accounts are affected, and by how much. Journals are kept in chronological order. A company can keep several journals such as sales journals, purchase journals, and general journals.
4. *Post to ledger.* Journal entries are transferred to the ledger accounts. The ledger is a record of all of the company's accounts. Unlike the journals, which are kept in chronological order, the journal is kept in account order.

At the end of the accounting period, there are also six steps that must be taken. These are:

1. *Trial balance.* This is a calculation to check that the sum of all debits equals the sum of all credits. Debits and credits must balance. When they do not, it is a sign that there has been an error at some point in the process. Errors can occur when posting journal entries to the ledger, transferring the ledger account balances to the trial balance columns, totaling the debits and credits, or posting credits or debits in specific columns. If a trial balance is not balanced, then the transactions must be reviewed to find the error so it can be corrected and the debits and credits can balance.
2. *Adjusting entries.* Here accrued and deferred items are prepared and posted to journals and ledger accounts. These are made only at the end of the accounting period. With accrued items, the company has realized the revenue or expense but has not yet had an actual transaction that would create the need for a journal entry. With deferred items, it is the opposite. The company has recorded a transaction as a journal entry, but has not yet realized the revenue or expense associated with it. Employee salaries and interest income are common accrued items. Prepaid insurance or rent are common deferred items.
3. *Adjusted trial balance.* This is a check, as in the first step, that the debits and credits balance.
4. *Preparation of financial statements.* These include the balance sheet, the income statement or P&L, the statement of retained earnings, and the statement of cash flow.
5. *Posting of closing entries.* These transfer balances from temporary accounts, such as the revenue account and the expense account, to the ledger accounts. Once the balances are transferred, the temporary accounts are considered closed. They do not appear on the balance sheet.
6. *After-closing trial balance.* Once the closing entries have been made, this step checks that the debits and the credits are still balanced.

THE GENERAL LEDGER

Let's take a look at the general ledger. This is a term that you will hear a lot related to your company's finances. The general ledger is where all accounting transactions are posted. It uses a double entry system with two columns for each transaction—one for debits and one for credits. The general ledger provides data that is used in the balance sheet and the P&L.

Here is an example of general ledger entries:

ACCOUNT 101

Cash—Regular Checking	*Debits*	*Credits*	*Balance*
			$ 3,305.00
10/15/07 Lighting 'N More Deposit	$12,800.00		16,105.00
10/21/07 Homestuff Order	7,200.25		23,305.25

ACCOUNT 401

Sales—Lamps	*Debits*	*Credits*	*Balance*
			$ 5,506.25
10/15/07 Lighting 'N More Order		$12,800.00	18,306.25
10/21/07 Homestuff Order		7,200.25	25,506.50

MEMO

RE: DEBITS AND CREDITS

A double entry accounting system uses two columns to record transactions: one on the left for debits and one on the right for credits. This system requires that each transaction be recorded with at least two entries, a credit and a debit, thereby creating a balance.

You probably think of debits only as decreases and credits only as increases. This is not necessarily so! In some cases, a debit can be an increase, just as a credit can be a decrease. The type of account determines whether a transaction is a decrease or an increase. In general, gains, income, revenue, and liability accounts are increased with a credit, whereas dividends, expenses, assets, and losses are increased with a debit. The opposite action decreases those accounts—gains, income, revenue, and liability accounts are decreased with a debit, whereas dividends, expenses, assets, and losses are decreased with a credit.

As you can see in this example, the debits in the cash account are balanced by credits of the same amount in the sales accounts. This is a requirement for the general ledger—the debits and credits must be balanced. In the example, the cash account is increased by the two debits and the sales account is increased by the two credits. This is because asset accounts, such as cash accounts, are always increased by debits and decreased by credits. In contrast, revenue accounts, such as sales accounts, are always increased by credits and decreased by debits.

Regardless of the method of accounting that your business uses, it will have to be consistently and accurately applied. By understanding a little of what goes on in the accounting process, you will be more aware of your actions and how they fit in the cycle.

CHAPTER TWELVE

Simple Statistics

In business, we keep track of how we perform. The set of numbers (daily sales or returns, for example) is called a data set. We can analyze data sets using statistical methods, and find useful information—statistics—that can tell us what we've done and help us to predict what may happen in the future.

This chapter provides an overview of the basic concepts of statistics.

MEAN

The mean is a basic statistic that describes the mathematical average of a data set. Here is the formula:

mean = sum of values ÷ number of values

Let's look at an example. Your company needs to find the average monthly travel and entertainment cost for all employees. For six months, the expenses were $23,500, $30,100, $32,700, $26,400, $28,900, and $35,500. To find the mean, or average, add all the expenses together and divide by the number of months:

mean = $177,100 ÷ 6
= $29,516.67 (when rounded to the nearest cent)

MEDIAN

The median is the middle value in a data set. To find it, put all the numbers in your data set in order from smallest to largest (or largest to smallest) and find the middle number. This is the median. If there is an even amount of numbers in your data set and therefore no middle number, take the sum of the two middle numbers and divide by two. This would be your median. Here is the formula when your data set contains an even number of values:

median = sum of middle values ÷ 2

MODE

The mode is a basic statistic that describes a different type of average. It represents the value or values occurring most often in a data set. If no value occurs more than once, the data set is said to have no mode.

Find the mode of this data set: 82, 97, 85, 79, 76, 73, 76

The easiest way to identify the mode is to sort the data from high to low (or low to high):

97, 85, 82, 79, 76, 76, 73

Now, you can see that 76 is the only number that occurs more than once, making it the mode of the data set.

RANGE

Range is a basic statistic that describes the degree of variety in your data set. A large range indicates a more varied data set, while a small range indicates that the data is very similar. Here is the formula:

range = largest value – smallest value

Here is an example. Let's say you manage a product line that consists of five products. The prices for the products are $12.99, $18.99, $7.99, $7.99, and $16.99. What is the range?

First, identify the largest value: $18.99. Now, look for the smallest: $7.99. Put these values into the formula:

range = $18.99 – $7.99
= $11

The prices for your product line have a range of $11.

VARIANCE

Finding the variance of a data set will allow you to calculate the standard deviation. Variance is the measure of the dispersion of a distribution, or the mean of the squared differences from the mean. Eek! The mathematical terms sound confusing, don't they? Well, a variance is a little tricky to compute, but you can do it. Here is how:

First, calculate the mean (average) of your data set. Then, for each number in your set, subtract the mean and square the result. (The results are squared so there are no negative numbers.) Now, calculate the mean of the squared differences. It may be hard to follow—so let's look at an example.

We'll assume that there are six members of a telemarketing team. They track the number of calls they make each week, and the totals are 90, 85, 86, 92, 75, and 82. The first step toward finding the variance is to find the mean.

$$\begin{aligned} \text{mean} &= \text{sum of values} \div \text{number of values} \\ &= 510 \div 6 \\ &= 85 \end{aligned}$$

The second step is to subtract the mean, 85, from each number in our set:

$90 - 85 = 5$
$85 - 85 = 0$
$86 - 85 = 1$
$92 - 85 = 7$
$75 - 85 = -10$
$82 - 85 = -3$

MEMO
RE: VARIANCE
Follow these four steps to calculate the variance:
1. Calculate the mean of the data set.
2. Subtract the mean from each number in your data set.
3. Square each result.
4. Calculate the mean of the results.
The mean is the variance of your original data set.

Now, square the results:

$5^2 = 25$
$0^2 = 0$
$1^2 = 1$
$7^2 = 49$
$-10^2 = 100$
$-3^2 = 9$

Calculate the mean of the squared results:

$$\begin{aligned} \text{mean} &= 184 \div 6 \\ &= 30.67 \text{ (when rounded)} \end{aligned}$$

The variance in our telemarketing example is approximately 30.67. Had there been 85 calls in each of the six weeks, the variance would have been zero because there would have been no variance from the mean.

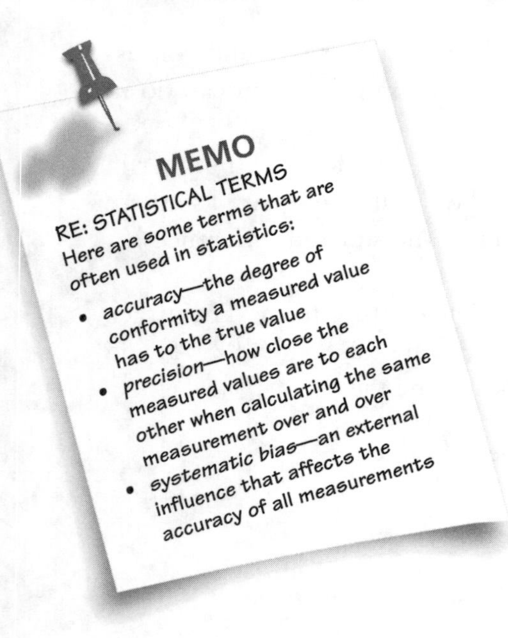

STANDARD DEVIATION

Standard deviation is a measure of how spread out, or how tightly clustered, the numbers are in a data set. It is a sort of mean of the mean. A large spread equals a large standard deviation. A small spread equals a small standard deviation.

Standard deviation is the square root of the variance. In our previous example, we found that the variance was 30.67. If we find the square root of that number, we will know the standard deviation. In this case, the square root of 30.67 is 5.538, which is then our standard deviation.

Remember that you always need to find the variance before you can calculate the standard deviation.

PRACTICE QUIZ

Use this data set to answer questions 1 to 4: age of employees: 24, 55, 60, 23, 45, 34, 37, 28, 37, 62, 24, 25, 37, 39, 48.

1. What is the range?
2. What is the mean?
3. What is the mode?
4. What is the median?

Use this data set to answer questions 5 to 10: unbillable hours per week, by employee: 10, 13, 11, 14, 15.

5. What is the range?
6. What is the mean?
7. What is the mode?
8. What is the median?
9. What is the variance?
10. What is the standard deviation?

Use this data set to answer questions 11 and 12: 233, 45, 200, 150, 50.

11. What is the variance for this data set?
12. What is the standard deviation?

CHAPTER THIRTEEN

Payroll Calculation

Employees are generally paid either a commission, an hourly wage, or a piecework rate. Most companies use a payroll system to process their payrolls, so you probably won't have to calculate it unless you work for a very small company. However, it can be helpful to understand the basic concepts of payroll—the ways that employees are paid and the types of withholdings, for example.

This chapter will provide you with an overview of payroll calculation. You will need to be aware, though, that every state has its own payroll and withholding requirements, so it is important to be aware of state regulations when calculating or working with payroll.

MEMO

RE: PAY FREQUENCY

If you are paid semimonthly, do you receive a paycheck twice a month or every other month? Not sure? Review these common pay frequency terms to be clear what is meant by each.

Daily—each day
Weekly—once per week
Biweekly—every other week
Semimonthly—twice per month
Monthly—once per month
Quarterly—once per quarter
Semiannually—twice per year
Annually—once per year

WHAT IS PAY?

It may seem obvious what constitutes pay, but in some situations it is not. There are certain items in a paycheck that are not technically pay. Pay includes:

- fees or wages
- bonuses
- holiday pay
- sick pay
- maternity or paternity leave pay (if your company offers it)

Some items that may be mistakenly considered pay because they could be included in a paycheck, but are not pay, include:

- expense reimbursements
- loans to employees
- tips
- pension or other retirement plan payments

INFORMATION ABOUT SALARIES

If you are involved in setting salaries for employees—or if you are interested in learning whether you are fairly compensated—there are many resources that provide salary information and ranges. Some of the online salary information may be a little too general for your needs, but it may at least give you a starting point from which you can modify the salary requirements. Some helpful online salary websites include:

- Salary.com: www.salary.com
- SalaryExpert.com: www.salaryexpert.com
- JobStar Central: http://jobstar.org/tools/salary/index.php

You can also check professional or trade organizations and associations for salary information. Many of them survey their members regularly to identify salary trends.

CALCULATING COMMISSION

Salespeople are most commonly paid commissions on completed sales; you may hear this referred to as "on commission." A commission is a percentage of the total sales generated by the employee. Commissions may be paid in addition to a salary or in place of one.

There are two primary types of commission: simple and accumulative. With simple commission, a salesperson is paid a commission as a percentage of the value of the product or service sold. For example, if a media sales representative is paid commission, she might receive 5% on all ads that she sells in a quarter. With accumulative commission, the commission rate increases with the amount of sales made. So, that same sales rep might have a compensation structure where she receives 3% for the first $20,000 in sales, 5% for sales between $20,000 and $40,000, and then 7% for sales above $40,000.

The formula for calculating commissions, whether simple or accumulative, is the same, but there is an extra step for calculating the accumulative form. At the most basic level, to calculate commissions you multiply the sales by the commission rate. So the formula looks like this:

$$\text{commissions} = \text{sales} \times \text{rate}$$

Let's look at an example: If the media sales rep is paid a straight 5% commission on all sales and she makes $57,000 worth of sales in the commission period, here is how you would calculate her payment:

$$\begin{aligned}\text{commissions} &= \$57{,}000 \times 0.05 \\ &= \$2{,}850\end{aligned}$$

So, the media sales rep would be paid $2,850 in commissions for the period.

If she is paid accumulative commission, you would calculate the commissions for the different rates and then add them together. Here is how you would calculate payment for the rep if she receives 3% for the first $20,000 in sales, 5% for sales between $20,000 and $40,000, and then 7% for sales above $40,000:

$$\begin{aligned}\text{commission rate 1} &= \$20{,}000 \times 0.03 \\ &= \$600\end{aligned}$$

$$\begin{aligned}\text{commission rate 2} &= \$20{,}000 \times 0.05 \\ &= \$1{,}000\end{aligned}$$

$$\begin{aligned}\text{commission rate 3} &= \$17{,}000 \times 0.07 \\ &= \$1{,}190\end{aligned}$$

Now, add the results for the three commission rates to find the total amount the media sales rep should be paid for the period: $600 + $1,000 + $1,190 = $2,790.

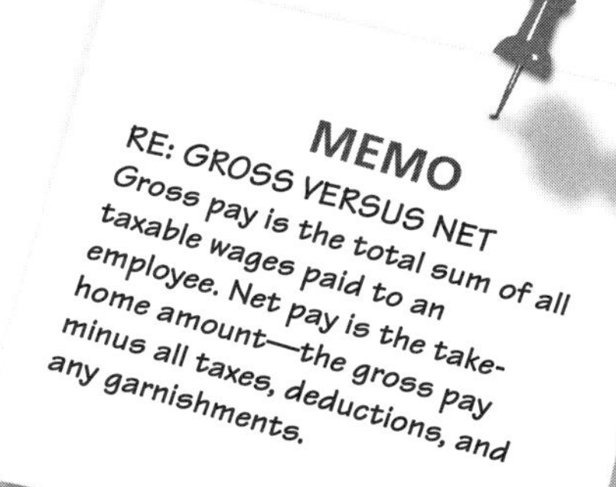

CALCULATING GROSS PAY USING HOURLY WAGES

Calculating gross pay using hourly wages is fairly straightforward. The formula is:

$$\text{gross pay} = (\text{regular rate} \times \text{regular hours}) + (\text{overtime rate} \times \text{overtime hours})$$

Say an employee is paid $12 per hour on a biweekly basis. He works 41 hours the first week and 51 hours the second week. For all overtime hours (those beyond 40 in a week), he is paid one and a half times his regular rate. What is his gross pay for this period?

Let's plug the numbers into our formula. Because he is paid biweekly, we know that the pay period is two weeks. So, the regular hours would equal 40 × 2 or 80:

$$\text{gross pay} = (\$12 \times 80) + (\text{overtime rate} \times \text{overtime hours})$$

He worked one hour overtime in the first week and 11 in the second. The total for the pay period is 12 hours of overtime. The rate of pay is $1.5 \times \$12$, or \$18 per hour:

$$\begin{aligned}\text{gross pay} &= (\$12 \times 80) + (\$18 \times 12)\\ &= 960 + 216\\ &= \$1{,}176\end{aligned}$$

The employee would be paid \$1,176 for the pay period.

CALCULATING GROSS PAY USING PIECEWORK RATE

Sometimes employees are paid according to the work that they produce. They receive a flat rate to produce a specific unit or a project. This is often the case for freelancers or contract employees. To calculate gross pay using the piecework rate, use this formula:

$$\text{gross pay} = \text{total number of pieces} \times \text{rate}$$

OVERTIME PAY

In general, if an employee is required to work overtime, then the employer must pay the employee more for that time. According to the U.S. Department of Labor's Fair Labor Standards Act, covered employees must receive overtime pay for all hours worked in excess of 40 hours in a workweek. The overtime rate must be at least one and a half times the regular rate of pay.

Because overtime pay increases the amount paid to employees, a company's bottom line could be affected if a great deal of overtime is required. This is often the case when companies do not plan for overtime when entering their salary line items in their budgets and financial plans. If you work in budgeting for a company where overtime may be expected, make sure that the overtime premiums are considered.

Let's look at how overtime can affect a budget.

Say you work for a marketing firm that has landed a new account. Your contract runs from July 15 to January 15 and you have an overall budget of \$600,000. Out of this budget, you will pay for all marketing materials, a radio ad campaign, trade shows, and your employees' hourly rates. When you and your team created your budget, you expected that the team would spend 2,880 hours working on this account at an average hourly rate of \$75. For two senior employees (who are exempt from overtime pay), the hourly cost is \$61 per hour. For two junior employees (who are eligible for overtime pay), the hourly cost is \$44 per hour (\$32 in wages and \$12 in benefits). Your budget assumed that half of the hours would be worked by the senior employees and half would be worked by the junior employees.

By November, however, things are getting backlogged. With a large trade show looming, two members of your team who are eligible for overtime pay have been working between 50 and 60 hours a week. For six weeks in November and December, the two employees each work an average of 18 hours of overtime every week for a total of 216 overtime hours. They are paid one and a half times their hourly rate.

At the end of the project, you compare your expenses with your budget and see the following:

- The project plan assumed 2,880 working hours: 1,440 hours by senior employees at a cost of $61 per hour and 1,440 hours by junior employees at $44 per hour. Total cost for the team: $151,200.
- The actual hours were 3,096 hours: 1,440 by senior employees at $61 per hour and 1,656 by junior employees—1,440 at $44 per hour and 216 at $60 per hour (overtime rate of $1\frac{1}{2}$ their hourly rate of $32, or $48 per hour, plus $12 per hour in benefits). Total cost for the team: $164,160.

With the overtime, your team cost $164,160, which is $12,960 more than you planned. This cuts into the profit for the project. Had overtime been planned for, you could have increased the estimate for the team and covered the cost to keep your profit the same.

PRACTICE QUIZ

1. Calculate the commission for a sales rep who made $452,000 in sales during a sales period and is paid a 6% rate on all sales.
2. An employee works 52 hours in a particular week. His hourly rate is $27.50 for a regular 40-hour workweek, and he receives one and a half times his pay for overtime. What would his gross pay be for the week?
3. Calculate the commission for an employee who makes $127,000 worth of sales in a period and is paid a 3% commission on the first $75,000 of sales, 4% commission on the next $50,000 of sales, and 5.5% commission on anything beyond.

PART three

Business Tools

CHAPTER FOURTEEN

Making the Most of Your Calculator

You may be looking at the title of this chapter and thinking, "What's so hard about using a calculator?" You add, subtract, multiply, and divide, right? Sometimes, you might even press the percent key. Well, if that is all you are using your calculator for, then this chapter will provide you with some tips to help you maximize an important business math tool!

In this chapter, we assume that you know how to use a calculator for the basic functions, so we cover only the most common complex functions.

CLEARING

There is nothing worse than entering a long series of numbers into a calculator, only to mistype one and have to start all over. Well, you don't necessarily have to start over. You can clear the last number entered on a calculator, although you cannot select previous numbers to clear.

To clear a number, first look to see which clearing setup your calculator uses: AC and C or C and CE. If your calculator has the AC and C buttons, you would click on C to clear your last entry. You would use AC to clear all the entries you have made. If your calculator has the C and CE buttons, you would use CE to clear your last entry and C to clear all the entries.

Let's work through some examples to show the difference between the two types of clearing.

First, say you entered the following into your calculator:

432 + 276 + 546 + **222**

But you meant to enter:

432 + 276 + 546 + **422**

Because the incorrect number was the last one that you entered, you would click on the C button (if your calculator uses C and AC) or the CE button (if your calculator uses CE and C) to clear only your last entry. All of the previous numbers that you entered will remain. After clearing your last entry, you can continue with your calculation.

If the incorrect entry was earlier in the series, you would have to clear all of the entries. For example, let's say you entered two more numbers before noticing your mistake:

432 + 276 + 546 + **222** + 731 + 600

But you meant to enter:

432 + 276 + 546 + **422** + 731 + 600

The incorrect number was not the last one entered, so you need to clear the whole series of numbers and start again. To do that, you would click the AC button (if your calculator uses C and AC) or the C button (if your calculator uses CE and C).

MEMO

RE: USING THE MICROSOFT OFFICE CALCULATOR

If your computer is equipped with Microsoft Office, you can use the calculator accessory to perform many functions, both simple and complex. To access the calculator, open the Accessories folder in Microsoft programs and then click on the calculator. The default view on this calculator is the basic, or standard, one, but you can change that by clicking on the View menu and selecting Scientific. The calculator will expand and you will need to choose a number system to use: hexadecimal, decimal, octal, or binary. The options available on the calculator will change depending on the number system you choose.

The Microsoft Office calculator can also be used for statistical calculations. It is a very handy function! To perform a statistical calculation, open the calculator in the Scientific view. Start by entering your first value (your piece of data), and then click on the "Sta" button. This will open the statistics box. Now, click on "Dat" (on the calculator) to save the value that you entered. It will be saved in the statistics box. Continue doing this until you have entered all of your data. Once your data entry is complete, you can click on "Ave" to get the average of all values entered, "Sum" to get the sum of all of the values, or "s" to get the standard deviation of the values.

MEMORY

If you are performing complex calculations, you may want to use the memory function to save parts for later use. There are four buttons related to memory on most calculators. These are:

1. MC: Memory Clear. This clears all numbers that have been stored in memory.

2. MR: Memory Recall. This recalls what has been stored in memory.
3. MS: Memory Store. This stores the displayed number in memory.
4. M+: Memory Add. This adds the displayed number to the number already in memory.

When memory is in use, an M will appear in the display box.

Let's take a look at some examples of how to use memory in your calculations. These exercises will be more helpful to you if you walk through them using your calculator. We'll compute $(55 \times 7) + (120 \div 8)$.

The first step is to make sure everything on your calculator is cleared out. Click on AC or C to clear all. Now, you can work through the problem:

1. Enter 55×7 and click =.
2. You should see 385 in the display bar. Click on MC to clear the memory and then click on M+ to add 385 to memory.
3. Now, click on AC (or C) to clear the last process.
4. Enter $120 \div 8$ and click =.
5. You should see 15 in the display bar. Click on +.
6. Click on MR to recall the 385 that you stored in memory. You should see 385 in the display bar.
7. Click on =.
8. You should see 400 (the sum of $385 + 15$) in the display bar.

1/*x* BUTTON

The $1/x$ button is a quick way of calculating 1 divided by any number. To use the button, enter any number and then click $1/x$. You do not need to click on the equal sign to get the result. For example, clicking on 2 and then $1/x$ shows that $\frac{1}{2}$ is equal to 0.5. Clicking on 8 and then $1/x$ shows that $\frac{1}{8}$ is equal to 0.125.

The $1/x$ button provides you with a very easy way to convert some simple fractions into decimal numbers.

x^2, *x*^3, *x*^*y* BUTTONS

These buttons allow you to raise a number to a particular power without having to hand enter all of the multiplication. Here is what the buttons mean:

x^2 = *x* squared
x^3 = *x* cubed
x^*y* = *x* to the *y* power (you enter the value of *y*)

To use the x^2 button, enter a number that you want to square and then click on the x^2 button. For example, click on 5 then x^2 and you will see 25 in the display bar. You do not need to click on the equal sign after clicking on x^2.

The process is the same for the x^3 button. Click on 5 then x^3 and you will see 125 in the display bar.

There is one additional step required for using the x^y button. This button allows you to raise a number to any power that you want. So, if you want to raise 5 to the sixth power, you would enter 5, then click on the x^y button, and then enter 6. For this, you do need to click on the enter button. Do that and you will see 15625 in the display bar. This is the result of raising 5 to the sixth power, or 5^6.

These buttons are very useful for calculating compound interest.

Pi BUTTON

Some calculators show the pi button as "pi," while others show it as the Greek letter π. Either way, clicking on it will display the value for pi, the ratio of the circumference to the diameter of a circle, approximately 3.14159. This button is a nice shortcut for entering the value of pi, especially if you have a hard time remembering what the value is!

n! BUTTON

The n! button calculates a factorial—the n factorial where n equals whatever number you enter. The exclamation point is the symbol for factorial, and n! means the product of all the whole numbers from 1 to n. So, 3! would mean $1 \times 2 \times 3 = 6$, and 5! would mean $1 \times 2 \times 3 \times 4 \times 5 = 120$. In the case of zero factorial, 0! is always equal to 1.

To use the button to calculate a factorial, enter the number for which you want to find the factorial and then click on the n! button. You do not need to click on the equal sign.

Sin, Cos, Tan BUTTONS

These buttons are used for trigonometry functions. You most likely won't have much use for them in regular business-related math, but it might be interesting to know how to use them. The functions are related to angles, and the buttons represent sine (the sin button), cosine (the cos button), and tangent (the tan button). To use the buttons, enter the degrees of the angle for which you wish to find the sine, cosine, or tangent, and then click on the corresponding button. You do not need to click on the equal sign.

For example, if you have an angle of 30 degrees and you want to know the sine of it, enter 30 and then click on the sin button. You should see 0.5 in the display bar.

Inv BUTTON

The inverse button, represented by inv, allows you to go backward to find the inverse of a given operation. For example, say you wanted to find the square root of 49. Here is how you would use the inv button to figure this out.

First, click on the inv button. Then, enter 49 as your value and click on the x^2 button. You should see 7 in the display bar. The square root of 49 is 7.

Here is another example. If you want to know the cube root of 512, click on the inv button. Enter 512 as your value and click on x^3. You should see 8 in the display bar because the cube root of 512 is 8.

After a calculation is complete, the inv button will turn off so you can move on to do other calculations as you normally would.

Dms BUTTON

This button converts values entered in decimal degrees format into degrees/minutes/seconds format, which is useful for measuring angles. This is also the format for coordinates for latitude and longitude. In degree/minute/second measurements, one degree is equal to 60 minutes and one minute is equal to 60 seconds. To use this feature, just enter a value and then click on the dms button. The converted value will appear in the display bar. For example, if you enter 8.48 and click on the dms button, the converted value will be 8.2848. This is read 8 degrees, 28 minutes, 48 seconds.

USING PARENTHESES

Using the parentheses on a calculator is easy to do. The hardest part is remembering to open and close them! Let's take a look at how to work through a problem using parentheses. Remember the formula for calculating depreciation using the units of production method? That is a perfect example of when using parentheses on the calculator can come in handy.

Here is the formula:

$$\text{depreciation amount} = (P - V) \times (U \div L)$$

where P = initial price
V = salvage value
U = units used in the current period (for example, a fiscal year)
L = expected lifetime units capacity of the asset

So, let's say you need to find the depreciation of a machine for the third year of its life. It was purchased for $25,000, has a salvage value of $3,000 and an expected useful life of 30,000 units, and produced 1,250 units in the current year. So, the problem looks like this:

$$\text{depreciation amount} = (\$25{,}000 - \$3{,}000) \times (1{,}250 \div 30{,}000)$$

To figure this out on your calculator, start by clearing all entries. Then, open the parentheses and type in 25,000 – 3,000 and close the parentheses. You should see 22,000 in the display bar. Click on × to multiply and open the next set of parentheses. Then, type in 1,250 ÷ 30,000 and close the parentheses. You should see 0.0416666 . . . in the display bar. Now, click on the equal sign and you should have the result: 916.67.

The depreciation amount is $916.67.

PRACTICE QUIZ

Use your calculator to answer the questions on this quiz.

1. Convert $\frac{1}{9}$ to a decimal number.
2. What is the cube root of 216?
3. Find the value of 22!.
4. Calculate 12^4.
5. What is the square root of 256?
6. Convert $\frac{1}{65}$ to a decimal number.
7. Find the value of 16!.
8. Calculate $(256 \div 8) + [(13 \times 3) \div 20]$.
9. What is the cube root of 4,913?
10. Calculate 4^3.
11. What is the square root of 81?
12. Calculate 7^5.
13. Calculate $(18 \times 6) - (45 \div 9)$.

CHAPTER **FIFTEEN**

Graphs and Charts

Graphs, charts, and tables are visual ways to organize and display information. You can use them to demonstrate relationships between quantities and to show patterns and trends in your industry. Because they are visual, they are often used in presentations and reports, allowing the author to convey information more quickly than if it is expressed in words. You should know how to accurately read and interpret data that is conveyed in tables, graphs, and charts, because they are widely used in most business settings.

This chapter demonstrates how to read a bar graph, line graph, pie chart, and table. It will also provide instructions for creating your own graphs, charts, and tables.

HOW TO READ A BAR GRAPH

A bar graph uses parallel bars, either vertical or horizontal, to show the relationship between two groups of related data—frequency data and grouped data. Look at the sample bar graph to understand the components.

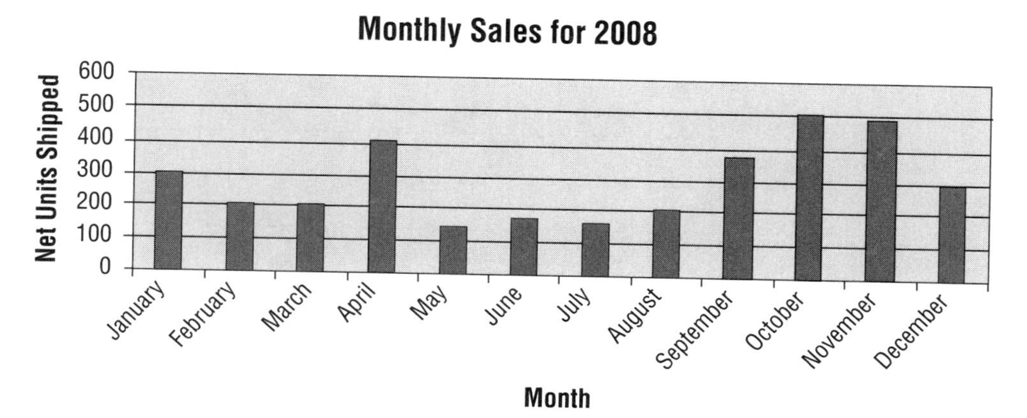

In this example, the graph's title is "Monthly Sales for 2008." Every graph should have a title to clearly identify what it represents.

Frequency Data Axis

The frequency data axis identifies the measure of the grouped data on the graph. In our example, the frequency data axis is titled "Net Units Shipped" and represents the number of units, starting at 0 and ending at 600.

Horizontal Lines

The horizontal lines represent the number of net units shipped.

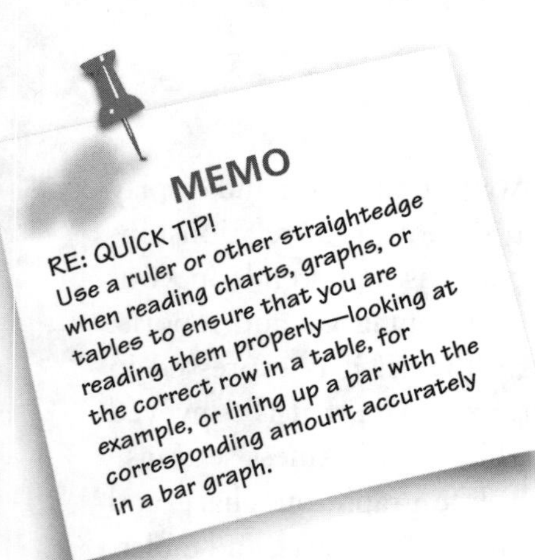

Grouped Data Axis

The grouped data axis identifies the data that is being measured on the graph. The grouped data axis is titled "Month" and displays the months that have been tracked, starting with January and ending with December.

Bars

The vertical bars in the graph measure the net units that were shipped each month. You can read the amount of each bar by looking at the horizontal lines that intersect the bars.

HOW TO READ A LINE GRAPH

A line graph uses points connected by lines to represent the relationship between two groups of related data. This type of graph works well to show trends and is best

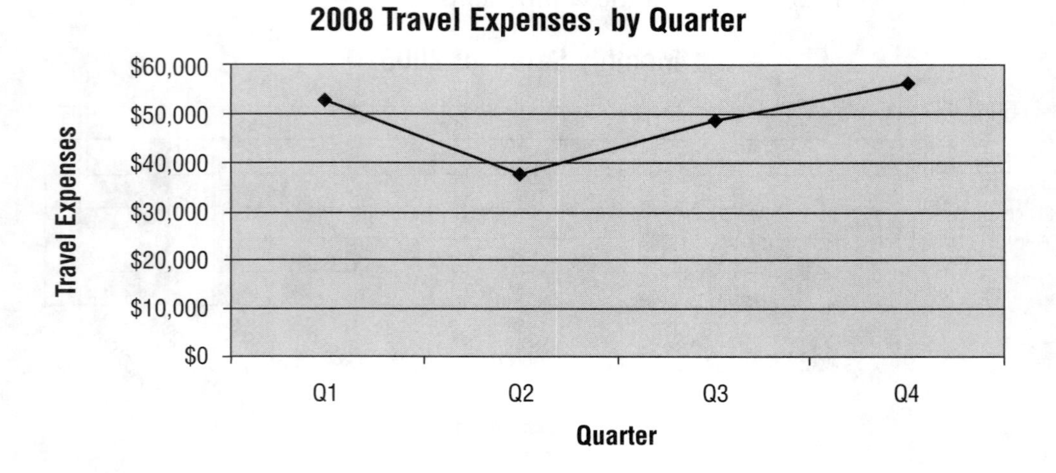

used when a period of time is involved. In the example titled "2008 Travel Expenses, by Quarter," you can see that the expenses dipped in the second quarter and then rose in the third and fourth quarters.

HOW TO READ A PIE CHART

A pie chart summarizes data and presents it as a percentage of a total. This type of chart should be used only when you want to show proportions. In the example titled "Number of Employees, by Department," each slice of the pie, shown in a different shade, represents a percentage of the total employees. The legend on the right shows which departments are represented by each shade. Looking at this chart, you can see that the sales department has the largest percentage of employees, at 20%. The next largest percentage is the production department with 19%.

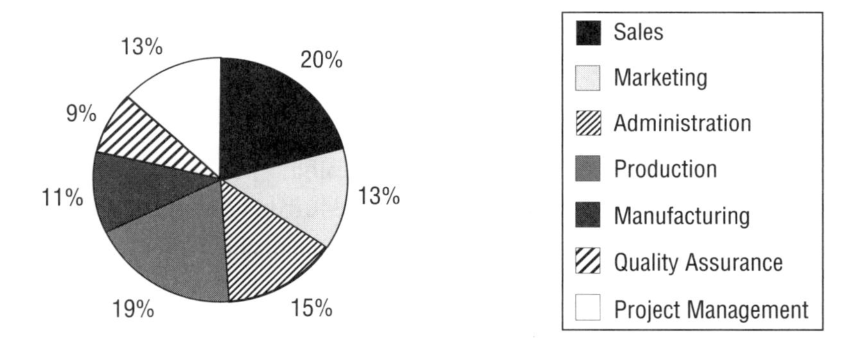

HOW TO READ A TABLE

A table displays a summary of data by category. The key to reading a table is to be sure that you are reading the correct column and row to find the information that you need. In a table, each column should have a heading to identify the information that each is presenting. In the example titled "Patients Seen, by Office Location," the leftmost (stub) column heading is Medical Group Doctor, and the other column headings are Free Clinic, Uptown Medical Center, and East End Clinic. Each row represents an individual medical group doctor and the number of patients seen by a particular doctor is presented in that row.

Patients Seen, by Office Location			
Medical Group Doctor	**Free Clinic**	**Uptown Medical Center**	**East End Clinic**
Dr. Walsh	15	15	29
Dr. Smith	30	25	15
Dr. Jones	20	25	17
Dr. Montana	28	30	13
Dr. Rose	10	41	22
Dr. Ellis	6	52	20
Total	**109**	**188**	**116**

CREATING EXCEL CHARTS

Excel makes creating charts and graphs easy. Using data that you have entered into Excel, you can create charts and graphs that you then import into a Word document, or keep in Excel.

To create a chart using Excel, enter your data and then highlight all of the data that you would like to include in the graph.

Click on the Chart Wizard button on the toolbar. You will be walked through four steps to create your chart. The first step requires you to select a chart type. The types of charts available include several standard charts such as pie, bar, and column charts and a set of more complex custom charts.

After you have selected your chart type, you will be prompted to identify the data (from your highlighted data) that will be used to create the chart. Then, give your chart a name and label the *x*-axis and *y*-axis. Once you have set up and labeled your chart, you can use it within the Excel spreadsheet where you have your data, or you can copy it to another document. Excel charts and graphs can be easily placed into Word documents or PowerPoint presentations, for example, just by copying and pasting as you would a block of text or an image.

If you save an Excel worksheet as an HTML file, Excel will automatically convert any charts to GIF (image) files.

LAY OUT FOR LEGIBILITY

When you are laying out your chart or graph, pay attention to its legibility. You can have great data, but if it is laid out poorly, it may not convey the proper message.

For example, if you have data for two product lines and you want to compare their monthly sales, you could lay out a bar graph in two different ways, one being much more usable than the other.

Let's look at two graphs that express the same data: monthly product sales for 2008.

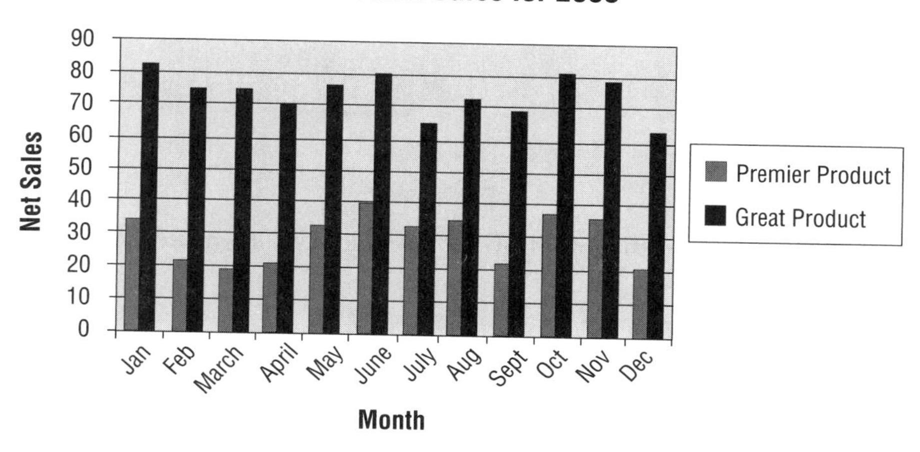

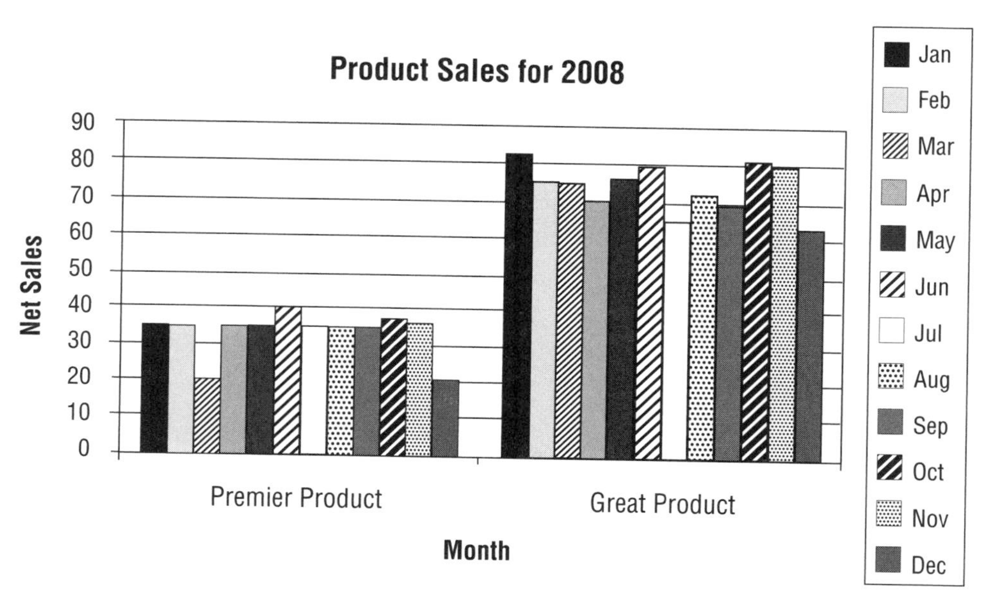

In the first graph, it is much easier to compare the monthly sales. The second graph requires far too much back-and-forth to compare the monthly sales by product.

If you think about how your readers will use your graph, it will help you to prepare one that shows your data clearly and accurately.

PRACTICE QUIZ

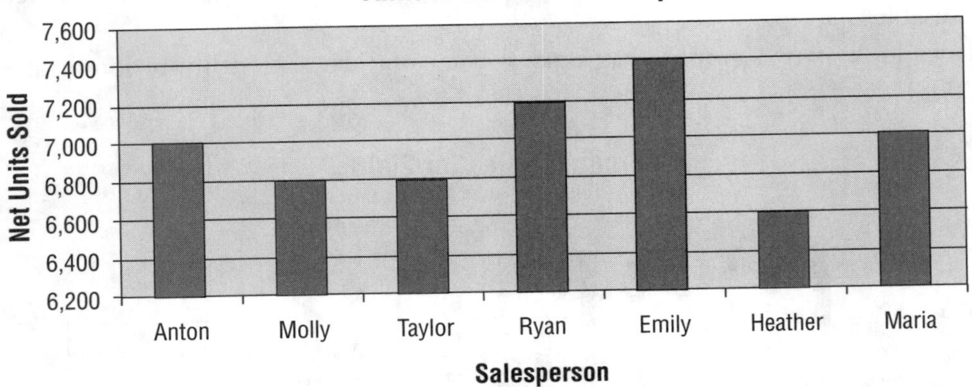

Using the data shown in the graph titled "Annual Sales Team Report," answer the following questions:

1. Which salesperson sold the most units?
2. What is the range in net units sold?
3. How many total units did the top two salespeople sell?
4. Which salesperson sold the fewest units?
5. How many units did Maria sell?
6. How many units were sold by all salespeople combined?

Cases of Smoothie Mixes Sold, by Store for 2008

Flavor	The Juice Stand	Barb's Bananas	Just Fruit! Shop and Café
Apple	1	2	1
Banana	10	20	5
Papaya	0	2	1
Strawberry	15	15	10
Blueberry	10	12	8
Mango	6	10	6
Total	**42**	**61**	**31**

Using the data shown in the table of smoothie mixes sold, answer the following questions:

7. How many smoothie mixes did The Juice Stand sell in 2008?
8. What was the highest-selling smoothie mix?
9. Which store sold the most smoothie mix?
10. Based on the data, which smoothie mix would you recommend be eliminated?
11. How many cases of strawberry and banana smoothie mixes were sold in total?

Practice Quiz Answers

CHAPTER 1

1. $60 + 89 =$ **149**
2. $126 + 38 =$ **164**
3. $539 + 348 =$ **887**
4. $866 + 229 =$ **1,095**
5. $17{,}776 + 7{,}432 =$ **25,208**
6. $38{,}967 + 12{,}453 =$ **51,420**
7. $55{,}188 + 27{,}339 =$ **82,587**
8. At the monthly production meeting, the warehouse manager reported that the following drop shipments had been received: 3,421 red units, 674 blue units, 1,801 green units, and 5,732 yellow units. How many total units were received? **11,628**
9. $128 - 13 =$ **115**
10. $140 - 29 =$ **111**
11. $667 - 73 =$ **594**
12. $12{,}892 - 13 =$ **12,879**
13. $21{,}300 - 12{,}299 =$ **9,001**
14. $81{,}562 - 9{,}341 =$ **72,221**
15. $9 \times 7 =$ **63**
16. $12 \times 12 =$ **144**
17. $18 \times 4 =$ **72**
18. $86 \times 21 =$ **1,806**
19. $371 \times 49 =$ **18,179**
20. $14{,}820 \times 27 =$ **400,140**

21. 23,892 × 50 = **1,194,600**
22. 567 × 15,637 = **8,866,179**
23. Annie receives a paycheck twice a month. Her take-home pay in each semimonthly paycheck is $1,605. What is her yearly take-home pay? **$38,520**
24. 28 ÷ 14 = **2**
25. 55 ÷ 11 = **5**
26. 426 ÷ 6 = **71**
27. 16,498 ÷ 4 = **4,124.5**
28. 32,335 ÷ 25 = **1,293.4**
29. 8,722 ÷ 80 = **109.025**
30. A company has 14 departments, all sharing equally the cost of new servers. The total cost for the servers is $48,628. What is each department's share? **$3,473.43**

Convert the following Roman numerals to Arabic numerals:
31. XVIII = **18**
32. CCXCV = **295**
33. MXCII = **1,092**

CHAPTER 2

1. $\frac{3}{8} + \frac{5}{12} = \frac{19}{24}$
2. $\frac{5}{6} + \frac{4}{6} = \frac{9}{6} = 1\frac{3}{6} = 1\frac{1}{2}$
3. $1\frac{1}{2} + \frac{1}{4} = 1\frac{3}{4}$
4. $\frac{3}{4} - \frac{1}{2} = \frac{1}{4}$
5. $\frac{4}{9} - \frac{13}{72} = \frac{19}{72}$
6. $\frac{5}{8} - \frac{9}{16} = \frac{1}{16}$
7. 10.34 × 9.2 = **95.128**
8. 142.3 × 3 = **426.9**
9. 127 × 0.548 = **69.596**
10. 348.52 ÷ 2 = **174.26**
11. 29 ÷ 0.33 = **87.879 (rounded)**
12. 2.470 ÷ 0.095 = **26**

Convert the following fractions to decimals:
13. $\frac{3}{5}$ = **0.6**
14. $\frac{2}{7}$ = **0.286 (rounded)**
15. $\frac{7}{8}$ = **0.875**
16. $\frac{8}{35}$ = **0.229 (rounded)**

Convert the following decimals to fractions:

17. 0.3 = $\frac{3}{10}$

18. 0.015 = $\frac{3}{200}$

19. 0.25 = $\frac{1}{4}$

20. 0.65 = $\frac{13}{20}$

CHAPTER 3

1. How many inches are in 16 feet? **192**
2. Convert 60 degrees Celsius to Fahrenheit. **140 degrees**
3. Forty-eight feet is equal to how many yards? **16**
4. How many feet are in three miles? **15,840**
5. Convert 95 degrees Fahrenheit to Celsius. **34.99 degrees**
6. Convert 300 millimeters to inches. **11.81**
7. Convert five miles to kilometers. **8.05**
8. How many feet are in 2.5 yards? **7.5**
9. How many ounces are in 6.5 pounds? **104**
10. Convert 70 degrees Fahrenheit to Celsius. **21.11 degrees**
11. Convert 15 degrees Celsius to Fahrenheit. **59 degrees**
12. What is the area of a square that has 11-inch sides? **121**
13. How many liters are in five pints? **2.37**
14. What is the area of a triangle with a base of 10 inches and a height of 7 inches? **35**

CHAPTER 4

1. What is 20% of 80? **16**
2. Convert 83% to a decimal. **0.83**
3. What is 38% of 50? **19**
4. Calculate the amount of sales tax on an item that sells for $49.99 using a 7% tax rate. **$3.50**
5. What percentage is 7 of 63? **11.11% (when rounded)**
6. What percentage is 12 of 90? **13.33% (when rounded)**
7. Convert 0.125 to a percent. **12.5%**
8. If 350 people were asked to participate in a marketing survey and 260 of them actually completed the survey, what percentage of those asked went on to complete the survey? **74%**
9. Convert 35.75% to a fraction. $\mathbf{\frac{143}{400}}$

10. The suggested retail price for a product is $29.95. If a retailer purchases 52 units at a 40% discount, what is the total cost of the order? **$934.44**
11. Convert $\frac{5}{8}$ to a percent. **62.5%**
12. If you sold 316 units last quarter, how many units would you need to sell to realize a 15% increase this quarter? **363.4**
13. Convert $\frac{9}{10}$ to a percent. **90%**
14. Calculate the return percentage: 435 units sold, 29 units returned. **6.67% (when rounded)**
15. Convert 5% to a fraction. $\mathbf{\frac{1}{20}}$

CHAPTER 5

1. An entrepreneur has applied for a $40,000 loan for her start-up business. Which set of terms would be the most cost-efficient for her? **b. a three-year loan at 6%, compounded monthly**
   - **a.** a three-year loan at 7%, compounded quarterly: **total due at end of period $49,257.57**
   - **b.** a three-year loan at 6%, compounded monthly: **total due at end of period $47,867.22**
   - **c.** a four-year loan at 6%, compounded annually: **total due at end of period $50,499.08**
2. A company borrows $10,000 for one year with a compounding interest rate of 5% per month. How much does the company pay back at the end of the loan period? **$10,511.62**

How much would you need to deposit to end up with $40,000 if the terms were as follows?

3. 4% interest, compounded monthly, for three years: **$35,483.90**
4. 6% interest, compounded quarterly, for five years: **$29,698.82**
5. 5% interest, compounded annually, for five years: **$31,341.05**

Calculate the simple interest for the following:

6. a $2,700 deposit for two years at 4.5% interest: **$243**
7. a loan of $55,000 for six months at 8% interest: **$2,200**
8. a loan of $15,000 for three months at 7.5% interest: **$281.25**

Calculate the compound interest for the following:

9. a $42,000 loan for five years at 9% interest, compounded quarterly: **$23,541.39**
10. a $22,000 deposit for two years at 4% interest, compounded monthly: **$1,829.15**
11. a $9,000 loan for one year at 6% interest, compounded monthly: **$555.10**

CHAPTER 6

Calculate the annual depreciation amount for the following items using the straight-line method:

1. a vehicle purchased for $37,500 that has a useful life of six years and a salvage value of $4,000: **approximately $5,583.33**
2. a photocopier with a useful life of three years, purchased for $880, with a salvage value of $100: **$260**
3. three computers purchased for $2,045 each, with useful lives of two years and a total salvage value of $425: **$2,430 ($810 for each computer)**

Calculate the annual depreciation amount for the following items using the units of production method:

4. a binding machine purchased for $83,000 with a salvage value of $12,000, lifetime unit production capacity of 750,000 bindings, and production of 18,550 bindings in the current year: **approximately $1,756.07**
5. a scanner with a lifetime capacity of 50,000 scans, purchased for $11,720, and having a salvage value of $3,450. It produced 1,060 scans in the current year: **approximately $175.32**
6. a fleet of six identical cars, each purchased for $25,200 and each with a useful life of 75,000 miles and salvage value of $6,300. In the current accounting year, car A had 12,305 miles, car B had 10,170 miles, car C had 14,201 miles, car D had 14,220 miles, car E had 12,992 miles, and car F had 11,550 miles. **Total: $19,010.37 (car A $3,100.86, car B $2,562.84, car C $3,578.65, car D $3,583.44, car E $3,273.98, car F $2,910.60). If you don't round the annual value of each individual car, the total is 1¢ more, $19,010.38.**

Calculate the annual depreciation amount for the following items using the sum of the years' digits method:

7. a generator with a purchase price of $7,399, a salvage value of $600, and a useful life of nine years. The generator is in its fourth year of service: **approximately $906.53**
8. that same generator in its seventh year of service: **approximately $453.27**
9. a vehicle in its second year of service with a useful life of five years and a salvage value of $3,800, purchased for $13,700: **$2,640**
10. that same vehicle in its fifth year of service: **$660**

Calculate the annual depreciation amount for the following items using the declining balance method:

11. a truck purchased for $41,500 with a salvage value of $9,000 and a current book value of $37,000. The expected useful life of the truck is seven years, and it is in its first year of service: **approximately $7,928.57**

12. a recording system purchased for $43,650 with a current book value of $21,500 and a salvage value of $9,000. It is in its sixth year of service and has a useful life of 15 years. **Be careful! Using the declining balance method, the depreciation amount is $2,150. However, the rule using this method is that the depreciation amount should not be less than if you used the straight-line method. So, if you check your work by calculating the depreciation using that method, you will find that the straight-line depreciation amount is $2,310. The answer is to use the straight-line method, or $2,310, rather than the declining balance method.**

Calculate the annual depreciation amount for the following items using the double declining balance method:

13. ten laptop computers purchased for $1,735 each. They each have a current book value of $800 and a salvage value of $200. They are in their second year of service with a useful life of four years. **$4,000 ($400 for each computer)**
14. a projector in its third year of service with a current book value of $2,200. It was purchased for $5,800 and has a salvage value of $900 and a useful life of 12 years. **As with the declining balance method, the double declining balance method of depreciation amount should not be less than if you used the straight-line method. In this case, the straight-line depreciation is $408.33 and the double declining balance method is $366.67, so you would use the straight-line method amount.**

CHAPTER 7

Use markup from cost for questions 1 to 8:

1. What is the markup rate on a computer that costs $722 and has a selling price of $1,199? **approximately 66%**
2. If the markup on a pen that costs $2.25 is $0.75, what is the markup rate? **approximately 33%**
3. What is the cost of a blouse that sells for $64 and has a markup rate of 76%? **approximately $36.36**
4. What is the cost of a product that sells for $55.44 and has a markup rate of 27.2%? **approximately $43.58**
5. What is the price per hour for a service that has a cost of $58.79 per hour and a markup rate of 80.9%? **approximately $106.35**
6. What is the selling price of an item with a cost of $50.51 and a markup rate of 6.7%? **approximately $53.89**
7. If the price of a bracelet is $89.10 and the cost is $28.44, what is the markup rate? **approximately 213%**

8. What price would you set for an item if your cost was $34.54 and you were using a markup rate of 52.5%? **approximately $52.67**

Use markup from price for questions 9 to 17:

9. What is the price of an item where the cost is $41.40 and the markup rate is 34%? **approximately $62.73**
10. What is the markup rate for an item with a cost of $24.99 and a price of $36.75? **32%**
11. If a company's markup rate is 31.7%, what would be the price of an item that has a cost of $10.87? **approximately $15.92**
12. What is the cost for an item that sells for $60.08 and has a markup rate of 32.2%? **approximately $40.73**
13. What is the price of a handbag with a cost of $66.65 and a markup rate of 76.9%? **approximately $288.53**
14. What is the markup rate for a fixed-price dinner with a cost of $49.50 and a menu price of $90? **45%**
15. What is a company's cost for an item that sells for $15.96 and has a markup rate of 24.5%? **approximately $12.05**
16. What is the cost of an item that sells for $100 and has a markup rate of 40%? **$60**
17. What is the markup rate for an item with a cost of $8.45 and a price of $30.70? **approximately 72.5%**

Use markdown for questions 18 to 23:

18. A sofa that had originally been priced at $900 was marked down by 20% and then by 30%. What was the final selling price? **$504**
19. If a wholesaler originally charged $60.35 per unit for an item and marked it down by 35.8%, what sale price would it offer retailers? **approximately $38.74**
20. If the sale price of a pair of jeans is $72.89 and the advertised markdown is 55%, what was the original price? **approximately $161.98**
21. What is the markdown rate if the original price of an item was $137.54 and the sale price is $64.65? **approximately 53%**
22. What is the sale price for a plate that originally was priced at $29.99 and has been marked down 73.5%? **approximately $7.95**
23. Find the markdown rate of an item that has a sale price of $27.17 and an original price of $89. **approximately 69.5%**

Use breakeven point for questions 24 and 25:

24. A company has set the price for an item at $30. The total fixed costs are $15,000 and the variable costs per unit are $17. What is the breakeven point? **1,154 units**

25. Will a company break even if it sells 10,000 units of a $15 product that has total fixed costs of $27,000 and variable costs per unit of $11? **Yes. The breakeven point is 6,750, so the company would more than break even if it sells 10,000 units.**

CHAPTER 12

Use this data set to answer questions 1 to 4: age of employees: 24, 55, 60, 23, 45, 34, 37, 28, 37, 62, 24, 25, 37, 39, 48.

1. What is the range? **39**
2. What is the mean? **38.5 (when rounded)**
3. What is the mode? **37**
4. What is the median? **37**

Use this data set to answer questions 5 to 10: unbillable hours per week, by employee: 10, 13, 11, 14, 15.

5. What is the range? **5**
6. What is the mean? **12.6**
7. What is the mode? **There is no mode.**
8. What is the median? **13**
9. What is the variance? **3.44**
10. What is the standard deviation? **1.855 (when rounded)**

Use this data set to answer questions 11 and 12: 233, 45, 200, 150, 50.

11. What is the variance for this data set? **5,875.44**
12. What is the standard deviation? **76.65 (when rounded)**

CHAPTER 13

1. Calculate the commission for a sales rep who made $452,000 in sales during a sales period and is paid a 6% rate on all sales. **$27,120**
2. An employee works 52 hours in a particular week. His hourly rate is $27.50 for a regular 40-hour workweek, and he receives one and a half times his pay for overtime. What would his gross pay be for the week? **$1,595**
3. Calculate the commission for an employee who makes $127,000 worth of sales in a period and is paid a 3% commission on the first $75,000 of sales, 4% commission on the next $50,000 of sales, and 5.5% commission on anything beyond. **$4,360**

CHAPTER 14

Use your calculator to answer the questions on this quiz.

1. Convert $\frac{1}{9}$ to a decimal number. **0.111 (when rounded)**
2. What is the cube root of 216? **6**
3. Find the value of 12!. **479,001,600**
4. Calculate 12^4. **20,736**
5. What is the square root of 256? **16**
6. Convert $\frac{1}{65}$ to a decimal number. **0.015 (when rounded)**
7. Find the value of 16!. **20,922,789,888,000**
8. Calculate $(256 \div 8) + [(13 \times 3) \div 20]$. **33.95**
9. What is the cube root of 4,913? **17**
10. Calculate 4^3. **64**
11. What is the square root of 81? **9**
12. Calculate 7^5. **16,807**
13. Calculate $(18 \times 6) - (45 \div 9)$. **103**

CHAPTER 15

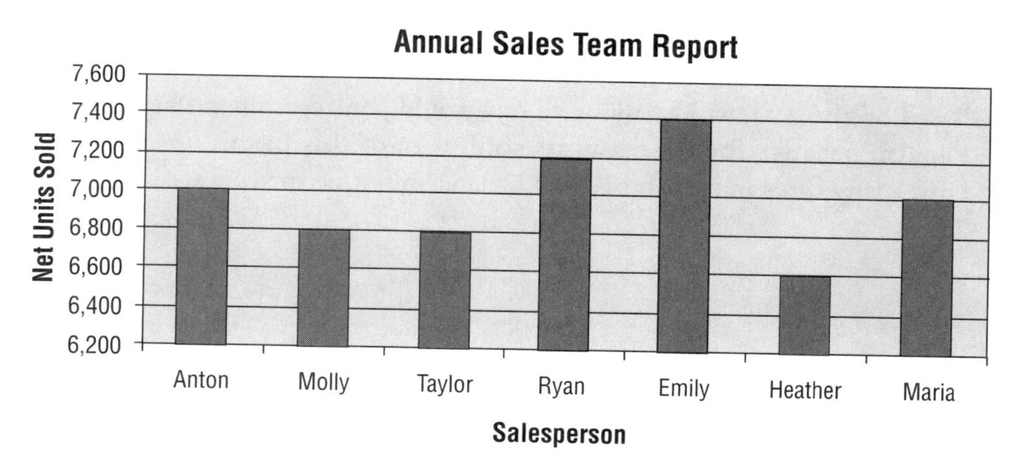

Using the data shown in the graph titled "Annual Sales Team Report," answer the following questions:

1. Which salesperson sold the most units? **Emily**
2. What is the range in net units sold? **800**
3. How many total units did the top two salespeople sell? **14,600 (the sum of Ryan's and Emily's sales)**
4. Which salesperson sold the fewest units? **Heather**

5. How many units did Maria sell? **7,000**
6. How many units were sold by all salespeople combined? **48,800**

Cases of Smoothie Mixes Sold, by Store for 2008			
Flavor	**The Juice Stand**	**Barb's Bananas**	**Just Fruit! Shop and Café**
Apple	1	2	1
Banana	10	20	5
Papaya	0	2	1
Strawberry	15	15	10
Blueberry	10	12	8
Mango	6	10	6
Total	**42**	**61**	**31**

Using the data shown in the table of smoothie mixes sold, answer the following questions:

7. How many smoothie mixes did The Juice Stand sell in 2008? **42**
8. What was the highest-selling smoothie mix? **Strawberry**
9. Which store sold the most smoothie mix? **Barb's Bananas**
10. Based on the data, which smoothie mix would you recommend be eliminated? **Papaya, because the fewest units sold were of this flavor.**
11. How many cases of strawberry and banana smoothie mixes were sold in total? **75**

Glossary

accounts receivable money owed to a company by its customers

accuracy how close a measured value is to the true value

add to bring two or more numbers together to make a new total

amortization the method of repaying a loan or debt by making periodic installment payments composed of both principal and interest. When all principal has been repaid, the load is considered fully amortized.

angle the figure formed by two line segments that have a common endpoint

annual Something that occurs every year

annual percentage rate (APR) the total or effective amount of interest charged on a loan, expressed as a percentage, on a yearly basis; value created according to a government formula intended to reflect the true annual cost of borrowing

ascending order arranged from smallest to largest

asset cash or a property or financial instrument that can be converted to cash, including stocks, bonds, real estate, and equipment

average the value obtained by dividing the sum of a set of quantities by the number of quantities in the set; also referred to as the mean

bar graph a way of showing data using horizontal or vertical bars so that the height or length of a bar indicates its value

benchmark a standard that is used for comparison

bias in statistics, the average difference between what has been measured or sampled and the truth. Bias can be caused by many different factors, such as favoring or encouraging some outcomes or answers over others, resulting in a distortion of the statistic, or it can be caused by surveying a nonrepresentative sample. Note that sampling errors from chance will likely cancel each other out, but those from bias will not.

borrowing a method of subtraction used when numbers are aligned in columns and the digit being subtracted is larger than the digit from which it is being subtracted. The method increases the digit that is being subtracted from by 10.

Borrowing works from right to left. Digits in the ones column borrow from digits in the tens column (the column immediately to the left of the ones column). Digits in the tens column borrow from digits in the hundreds column, digits in the hundreds column borrow from digits in the thousands column, and so forth.

breakeven point the point where a company's net sales just equals its costs

budget an itemized plan of a company's income and expenses over a specific period of time in the future

capacity the greatest volume that a container can hold

capital money or goods used to create income; the net worth of a business as represented by the amount by which its assets exceed its liabilities

cash actual currency—the amount of money in a company's bank accounts and items that can be converted for cash, such as checks and money orders

circumference the distance around a circle

common denominator two or more fractions that have the same denominator (the number below the line) are said to have a common denominator. Fractions can be added only when they have a common denominator.

common factor number that is a factor of two or more given numbers

cost of goods sold (COGS) all of the variable expenses related to the sale of a product. COGS includes the direct costs of production (such as raw materials) but not indirect costs (such as administrative costs). Cost of goods sold can also be referred to as cost of sales.

current assets those assets that a company could convert into cash or use within an operating cycle of the business (typically, one year). Current assets are listed on the balance sheet. Those assets can also be referred to as liquid.

current liabilities a liability is something that a business must pay. Current liabilities are those that a company expects to pay within an operating cycle of the business (typically, one year).

current ratio current assets divided by current liabilities

data a set of facts, statistics, or pieces of information

decimal a number that is written using base 10

decimal point the dot used to separate the whole number part from the fractional part of a decimal number

decimal system the numerical system that is commonly used worldwide. The units of this system of counting and measurement are powers of 10.

degree a unit for measuring angles and temperature

denominator the number below the line in a fraction that indicates into how many equal parts the whole is divided

depreciation a noncash expense that reduces the value of an asset as a result of wear and tear, age, or obsolescence

descending order arranged from largest to smallest
diameter the distance across a circle through its center
difference the amount that is left after one number is subtracted from another
digit an element within a system of numbers
dimension a measurement of length in one direction (i.e., height, width, depth)
dividend a number that is divided by another number
divisor the number used to divide another
earnings revenues minus the cost of sales, operating expenses, and taxes over a set period of time; also referred to as income
equation a mathematical sentence that contains an equal sign
equivalent having the same value
even number an integer that can be divided exactly by 2. The last digit in an even number will always be 0, 2, 4, 6, or 8.
exponent the number of times a number or an expression is multiplied by itself. An exponent is also referred to as the power, so 3^3 can be read as "Three to the third power" and means the same as $3 \times 3 \times 3$ (3 multiplied by itself twice).
factors the numbers that are multiplied together to get another number
fraction a number that names a part of a whole or a part of a group, expressed as part/whole
general and administrative expense overhead expenses not directly associated with the sale of a product, such as salaries, rent, telephone, and supplies
gross before deductions
gross margin a percentage that expresses gross income divided by net sales, or revenue minus COGS
gross weight the total weight of a unit, including contents, packaging, and all other materials
inventory the value of the products a company has on hand for resale to its customers. Inventory includes not only finished goods, but raw materials and goods in production as well.
least common denominator the least common multiple of the denominators of two or more fractions
least common multiple the smallest multiple that two or more numbers have in common
markdown the reduction in price of a product or service based on a percentage of the original price
markup the amount of money above the cost of a product or service that a business will charge for that product or service
mass the amount of matter in an object. Mass is related to weight.

mean the value obtained by dividing the sum of a set of quantities by the number of quantities in the set; also referred to as the average

median the middle number or the average of the two middle numbers in an ordered set of data

mode the number (or numbers) that occur(s) most frequently in a set of data

net earnings the profit earned by a business, after subtracting all expenses, depreciation, taxes, and so forth

net operating profit gross margin minus selling and administrative expenses

net sales the amount of sales generated by a business after allowing for returns, damaged or missing goods, and discounts

net weight the weight of a unit's contents, not including any packaging

net working capital current assets minus current liabilities

numerator the number above the bar in a fraction that shows how many equal parts of the whole are being considered

operating expenses fixed expenses, such as rent, utilities, and insurance

operating income a measure of a company's earning power from ongoing operations. Operating income is equal to earnings before the deduction of interest payments and income taxes. It can also be referred to as operating profit or EBIT (earnings before interest and taxes).

operation a mathematical process that combines two or more numbers. The fundamental operations of arithmetic are addition, subtraction, multiplication, and division.

other income income produced from something other than the normal operations of a business, such as investment interest, rent income, foreign exchange gains, and the sale of noninventory assets

percent per hundred; *percent* indicates the ratio of a number to 100. The symbol "%" indicates percent.

perimeter the distance around a closed plane figure, such as a square, triangle, and so on

precision how close the measured values are to each other when calculating the same measurement over and over

principal the amount of money borrowed or saved

profit and loss (P&L) statement a financial statement that summarizes the revenues, costs, and expenses incurred during a specific period of time—usually a fiscal quarter or year. These records provide information that shows the ability of a company to generate profit by increasing revenue and reducing costs. The P&L statement is also known as a statement of profit and loss, an income statement, or an income and expense statement.

radius the distance from the center of a circle to any point on the circumference of the circle

range the difference between the greatest and least numbers in a set of data

rate quantity of something measured per units of something else, thus describing a relationship between the two

ratio the comparison of two numbers by division

reciprocal one of two numbers whose product is 1. Two numbers are considered reciprocals of each other if their product equals 1.

revenue total income received for a product or services. For a company, revenue is the total amount of money that is received for goods sold or services provided during a particular time period. Revenue is calculated before expenses are subtracted.

salvage value the estimated value that an asset will have at the end of its useful life. This value is used to calculate depreciation amounts.

selling expense expenses related to order taking and product sales

simple interest a fixed percentage of the principal, paid yearly

simplify to express an answer in reduced form, or to use the rules of arithmetic to write an expression or fraction in condensed form

standard deviation the square root of the variance. Standard deviation shows how tightly clustered or spread out a set of data is.

sum the answer to an addition problem

variance the average of the squared differences from the mean

volume the amount of space occupied by an object

whole numbers the set of numbers that includes zero and all of the nonnegative integers but not fractions or numbers with decimal extensions. Whole numbers are often referred to as counting numbers or natural numbers.